Hope:

FACING THE MUSIC ON NUCLEAR WAR AND THE 1984 ELECTIONS

Books by Ground Zero

Nuclear War: What's in It for You?
What About the Russians—and Nuclear War?
Hope: Facing the Music on Nuclear War and the 1984 Elections

Published by POCKET BOOKS/LONG SHADOW BOOKS

Hope:

FACING THE MUSIC ON NUCLEAR WAR AND THE 1984 ELECTIONS

Ground Zero

Illustrations by
Matt Freedman

LONG SHADOW BOOKS
PUBLISHED BY POCKET BOOKS NEW YORK

Another *Original* publication of LONG SHADOW BOOKS

 A LONG SHADOW BOOK published by
POCKET BOOKS, a division of Simon & Schuster, Inc.
1230 Avenue of the Americas, New York, N.Y. 10020

ISBN: 0-671-50226-3

First Long Shadow Books printing December, 1983

10 9 8 7 6 5 4 3 2 1

LONG SHADOW BOOKS and colophon are
trademarks of Simon & Schuster, Inc.

Printed in the U.S.A.

For all the people raised on the story of the little train that puffed "I think I can, I think I can" right to the top of the mountain.

And for all human beings everywhere who understand that in the Nuclear Age hope lies in our willingness to face the music—and dance.

Contents

Preface

REASON TO BELIEVE

In giving this book the title *Hope,* we are proclaiming two separate but related truths.

The first is that no matter how uncontrollably the world seems to be drifting toward the unprecedented tragedy of nuclear war, it doesn't *have* to happen. It's not too late to "dance this mess around" if *all* of the people who have the power to change things will exercise it. That's right. There *is* a reason to believe.

The second is that *we*—the citizens of the United States—by virtue of our democratic political system, our historic pragmatism, *and* our huge arsenal of nuclear weapons are the world's best hope for leading humanity away from the precipice of annihilation. If not us, who?

As "facing the music" suggests, the hope required to meet this biggest-ever challenge is not a matter of crossing your fingers, wishing on a star, or praying. The hope we have in mind—the hope we want to kindle in *your* mind—is the kind of hope that comes from a rational understanding that nuclear war can be prevented and the comprehension of what you can do to help achieve this goal. It is therefore hope plus determination, the essential basis of constructive action.

And some constructive action is necessary. As this book goes to press, our species is thirty-eight years and 50,000 nuclear weapons into the Nuclear Age. (Do a little multiplication for the future of those numbers.) We—*homo sapiens*—are clearly facing the biggest problem we have *ever* faced—whether you think the wonderful miracle of life all began five thousand, five billion, or umpteen trillion years ago somewhere on the other side of the Big Bang.

YOU GOTTA HAVE HEART

Generally, we've written this book for all the millions of Americans who are starting to understand that the war after which "the living will envy the dead" may be becoming more likely—but who don't believe there's much they can do about it.

And we've especially written it for all the kids who have seen the headlines and watched the news and are talking among themselves about how short their lives could turn out to be.

GET READY

What this book is, then, is the truth, the whole truth, and nothing but the truth. Partly a you-can-do-it pep talk and partly the introduction of a game plan by which you can help prevent nuclear war, it's been designed to give you a solid *commonsense* understanding of both the nuclear war issue and how you can work out its problems through the ready-and-waiting vehicle of American democracy. It's also been designed to give you a kick in the tail and to make it clear that if you and lots of other people like you don't start working on this particular problem *right now,* your kids and your kids' kids and all those present and future "human beans in their designer jeans" may never get the chance to ask the question, "Why?"

And right now happens to be a *great* time to go to work on this problem. The 1984 election campaign presents one of those too-infrequent opportunities you have to confront the men and women who seek to represent *you* and *your* interests in your nation's capital—and to tell them that before you vote you'd like to know exactly what they have in mind. You can help create a constructive and thorough public (that's you) debate on this nation's overall strategy for preventing nuclear war.

Don't you think it's time? There have been eight previous presidential elections in the Nuclear Age. And we—the public—score zero to eight in taking advantage of the opportunity to confront and debate the nuclear war issue with our candidates for national office—and especially with our candidates for commander in chief. The prevention of nuclear war has never been a dominant campaign issue in presidential campaigns, and insofar as it has been discussed at all, it has suffered from the general tendency of political campaigns to simplify issues into catchy slogans such as those about bomber gaps and missile gaps.

The 1984 campaign can be—must be—different.

GIVE IT ALL YOU GOT

Don't dread what's coming ahead. The music isn't as tough to face as you might expect.

We've broken the big problem of preventing nuclear war down into six smaller and more tractable problems. The solutions to these six problems can bar the path to nuclear war as effectively as good firebreaks cut through the woods can halt the spread of raging forest fires. In fact, we call them the six "firebreaks" problems. Needless to say, they are *tough* problems.

We will describe just what these firebreak issues are, provide some critical bits of hard information about them, and then suggest some questions you should be asking yourself and the candidates for national office about how to solve them.

We have *not* provided the answers to these questions. It's your life that's at risk and it's your right as an American citizen—as well as your responsibility—to decide what makes the most sense.

What we *have* done is a lot like what the White House staff does for the president when it's decision-making time. They present him with an "options paper" that defines the problem, provides some relevant background information, and outlines a set of alternative approaches for finding a solution. The president mulls the problem over, weighs the pros and cons of the various options, and checks one of the boxes. Then everyone charges off to see if the new approach works—if it is a new approach.

For *each* of the firebreaks problems we have indicated what the possible approaches might be. Once you decide which approach to each of the firebreaks is most promising, you will have put together your own "how to prevent nuclear war" policy package.

But don't rush your judgment. These are not easy problems and you may want to see more information before you decide what needs to be done. For this purpose, we've suggested some next-level-of-education resources in "When You're Hot, You're Hot" at the back of the book.

What you should get from this book is enough of a grip on the nuclear war issue to be an "enlightened consumer" of campaign rhetoric in the 1984 elections. If you and enough other Americans refuse to settle for superficial answers to the most important questions of our time—or of any other era of human history, for that matter—then all those people who want to be *your* president (or *your* senator or *your* representative) are going to have to state concretely and coherently what they would do to prevent nuclear war. That would be refreshing—and pleasing to those guys who wrote "We the people . . ."

THE "IN" CROWD

In order to ensure that the material presented in this book is as balanced and as easy to understand as possible, we have invited a panel of four distinguished thinkers to assist us in the effort. Mr. Vanderkopf and Ms. Higgs have reviewed the various sections of the book, and portions of their dialogue and individual comments have been included in the text. Mr. Kuznetsov and Mr. Morton have limited their comments to the topic of U.S.–Soviet relations.

We would like to take this opportunity to express our gratitude to the members of the panel for their time and their insights and to formally introduce them to our readers with some relevant biographical information.

NAME: Rupert Ludwig Vanderkopf

CITIZENSHIP: U.S. (naturalized)

AGE: 38

SPECIES: *Struthio camelus* (Mr. Vanderkopf is an ostrich)

NUTSHELL VIEW ON THE THREAT OF NUCLEAR WAR: "I know it's becoming more likely, but I've got problems of my own."

BEHAVIORAL CHARACTERISTICS: Low key and agreeable until confronted with unpleasant facts, at which point he tends toward despair or hysteria. His extreme resistance to change is evidenced by the extraordinary amount of time he spends with his head in the ground, but he does exhibit some ability to adapt when the nature of the changes and the benefits of adapting to them (e.g., survival) are explained logically and in detail. The major difficulty is getting his attention in the first place.

HOBBIES: Sunbathing, building sand castles, wishful thinking, nonchemically induced oblivion

FAVORITE QUOTATION: "What, me worry?" (Alfred E. Newman, 195?)

FAVORITE ROCK 'N' ROLL SONG: "Boogie Oogie Oogie" (Taste of Honey, 1978)

NOTES: Mr. Vanderkopf was initially reluctant to serve on the *Hope* review panel—or, indeed, to take on the issue of nuclear war at all—due to the "pressing obligations of my business." Lots of people say that.

NAME: Ivan (Vanya) Pavlovich Kuznetsov

CITIZENSHIP: U.S.S.R.

AGE: 47

SPECIES: *Homo sapiens*

NUTSHELL VIEW ON THE THREAT OF NUCLEAR WAR: "As the whole world knows, it's all the Americans' fault, and if they mess with us they're gonna be sorry."

BEHAVIORAL CHARACTERISTICS: Mostly kind to his family and friends, but mistrustful of and hostile to almost everyone else, especially foreigners. Appears to be a classic case of what is known as the "them-against-us" mentality. Notably stubborn, especially in acknowledging and adapting to changes in his universe.

HOBBIES: Hockey, soccer, vodka, and muscle flexing

FAVORITE QUOTATION: "One sword keeps another in the sheath." (George Herbert, 1651)

FAVORITE ROCK 'N' ROLL SONG: "We Are the Champions" (Queen, 1978)

NOTES: Mr. Kuznetsov wishes to state for the record that he valiantly resisted selecting a song from "the trashcan of decadent Western rock and roll," and ultimately did so only because he feared refusal would be used as "another specious capitalist rationale for keeping valid Soviet views from the American public."

NAME: Charles (Chuck) David Morton

CITIZENSHIP: U.S.

AGE: 47

SPECIES: *Homo sapiens*

NUTSHELL VIEW ON THE THREAT OF NUCLEAR WAR: "As the whole world knows, it's all the Russians' fault, and if they mess with us they're gonna be sorry."

BEHAVIORAL CHARACTERISTICS: Mostly kind to his family and friends, but mistrustful of and hostile to almost everyone else, especially foreigners. Appears to be a classic case of what is known as the "them-against-us" mentality. Notably stubborn, especially in acknowledging and adapting to changes in his universe.

HOBBIES: Baseball, football, beer, and muscle flexing

FAVORITE QUOTATION: "To be prepared for war is one of the most effectual means of preserving peace." (George Washington, 1790)

FAVORITE ROCK 'N' ROLL SONG: "We're a Winner" (Impressions, 1968)

NOTES: Mr. Morton wishes to state for the record that he agreed to pick a favorite song from the canon of rock 'n' roll only because he suspected that "if I don't, these soft-heads will only use it as an excuse to cut out the eye-opening comments of a right-thinking American"—and because his kids insisted on it.

NAME: Clarity Jane Higgs

CITIZENSHIP: U.S.

AGE: 16

SPECIES: *Homo sapiens*

NUTSHELL VIEW ON THE THREAT OF NUCLEAR WAR: "No matter who got us into this mess, it's *all* of our lives that are at stake and *all* of us should be looking for a way out. And if we just sit on our tails with our fingers crossed, we're *all* eventually gonna be very sorry."

BEHAVIORAL CHARACTERISTICS: Generally an optimistic "can do" kind of person; can become quite impatient with people who aren't. Tendency to question authority when things don't make sense to her. Could probably be a little more respectful of her elders. Predisposed to rational dialogue, but sometimes waxes emotional.

HOBBIES: Music, dancing, and "the education of ostriches and persons of the Neanderthal persuasion in the art of survival in the Nuclear Age"

FAVORITE QUOTATION: "No problem of human destiny is beyond human beings." (John F. Kennedy, 1963)

FAVORITE ROCK 'N' ROLL SONG: "We Can Work It Out" (Beatles, 1966)

NOTES: It was Ms. Higgs who suggested incorporating the concept of "facing the music" and using song titles in the text. She also took it upon herself to select the titles used, which accounts for the preponderance of rock music citations, including "a few Golden Oldies for you Oldies but Goodies." Ms. Higgs has been overheard at social events arguing that the three most important questions in the universe are: (1) Where did we come from? (2) Where are we going? and (3) Do you believe in rock 'n' roll?

Did you really think that we would subject you to the measured utterances of traditional "experts"?

Which brings us to our final report. Working on the theory that primary education on nuclear war doesn't *have* to be boring—scary is bad enough—we have attempted to liven up the "big picture" of the problem of nuclear war and what you can do about it with the just-introduced fictional commentators, some pretty nifty drawings, a few parables, and a generally informal tone. As it turns out, these devices have proven to be useful in making specific points, but what we really hope is that some of them will make you grin a little and will thus break the tension as you go through the inevitably stressful process of learning how to help prevent nuclear war.

If you don't find our approach entertaining, please try to read the whole book anyway. You're certain to learn a lot—and your life may depend on it.

CAROLE JACOBS
ROGER MOLANDER

November 1983

Hope:

FACING THE MUSIC ON NUCLEAR WAR AND THE 1984 ELECTIONS

1

HAVE YOU HAD A VISION?

Highlights of World History,
April 25, 1985—December 31, 1999

CLARITY: This is one version of a story I want to be able to tell my children.

Looking back over the remarkable last fifteen years of this century, it's impossible to say that any one specific event marked the beginning of the change. We know for sure that in the 1984 presidential election, the concern of the American people had sparked an unprecedented debate on how to approach the prevention of nuclear war—a debate that the rest of the world followed avidly. Still, there were so many separate chains of causality, so many things occurring that seem to have been the result of sheer serendipity, so many decisive words that might have sprung from passing emotion rather than the considered decisions of great governments—we just can't be sure what started the change.

Of course, we'd all like to think that what really happened was a sort of global epidemic of sanity—humanity finally coming to its senses. But on an issue like nuclear war, humanity can only come to its senses one person at a time.

THUNDER AND LIGHTNING

It was April 25, 1985—the fortieth anniversary of the opening of the international conference that established the United Nations. Because both the President of the United States and the General Secretary of the Soviet Union were to address the United Nations General Assembly in New York that day, regular television programming around the world had been preempted to allow live broadcast of the speeches.

As the program began, however, nobody had much hope that what had once been planned as a celebration of world order was going to work out that way. Relations between the superpowers were at an all-time low, and many journalists and other observers were predicting yet another bitter superpower confrontation. In fact, there were even rumors that the start of the proceedings would be delayed because of some confusion or controversy about which head of state would speak first. It appeared that the two most powerful leaders in the world could not even agree on the order of their speeches!

Finally, the first speaker was introduced and began his prepared remarks. At first his words were measured and seemingly reasonable, but before long the speech took on a character that was all too familiar. It was yet another "We have done no wrong; they have done no right" polemic, complete with veiled threats about what might happen if "the struggling nations of the Third World are not permitted to establish the governments of their choice, free from the direct or indirect intervention of an arrogant power that insists the whole world be created in its image."

It was the same basic speech that has been delivered millions of times throughout human history—business as usual.

MOMENT OF TRUTH

As the second speaker climbed slowly to the podium, the close-up cameras showed his face, famous for its habitual expression of vigorous determination, to be pale and deeply shadowed. He shuffled through his papers for a few moments, then put them aside and began to speak. And this, translated into fifty languages and broadcast live by satellite to seven hundred million people, is what he said:

"Mr. Secretary, Ambassadors of the United Nations, people of the world: In the past ten days I have been party to two extremely disturbing events. You no doubt have heard rumors about the first, which I will confirm. Last Tuesday, the satellite system which provides early warning of attack upon my country malfunctioned in some way we have not yet diagnosed. Under the misapprehension that a massive nuclear first strike was imminent, I put the nuclear forces at my disposal on the highest level of alert. Our government leaders and my family were evacuated from the capital by helicopter, virtually all of our alert-status long-range bombers took to the air, and we were within minutes of launching our intercontinental ballistic missiles when the error was discovered.

"This near tragedy occurred in the middle of a particularly joyous family gathering. My daughter had come to visit and to give her mother and me the news that after many years of marriage she was pregnant with her first child. The alarm came as we were sitting down to dinner, and my daughter was evacuated with the rest of my household. But she was so upset by the false alarm that she returned to her own home early the next morning.

"Then, last Friday"—he paused and gripped the podium, and the world watched as one of its most powerful leaders struggled to control his emotions—"then, last Friday my daughter—without saying anything to her husband or to her mother or me—went to a clinic and had the child she was carrying aborted. My first grandchild is not to be.

"The conversation in which she told me what she had done was one of the saddest of my life. Having hoped so many years for a child, my daughter said she had decided that she could not bring one into a world that seemed intent on its own destruction. She said that children are the crucibles and living symbols of our hope for the future and that she had ceased to have any hope for a world that has evolved into a state of such profound madness.

"And so it is that I have come here today to tell you that we—the people of the world—cannot go on as a self-endangered species. It *is* madness and it must be stopped.

"I can tell you truthfully that I inherited, with the mantle of power, the responsibility to safeguard my country from foreign threat and the nuclear arsenal with which to do so.

"I can tell you truthfully that I did not personally create this hideous impasse which menaces hundreds of millions of lives and maybe even life itself.

"I can tell you truthfully that I have spent long nights agonizing about how to begin turning the world away from the path we have been following lemminglike toward oblivion, but that I have not discovered a way to do so without alarming those of my countrymen who think that the very survival of our nation lies in accumulating weapons that are equal or superior to those of any other nation.

"And I must also tell you that I see no probability, in the course we are on, of reversing the cycle of increasing fear and mistrust between the superpower nations and the increasingly monstrous weapons which are its product.

"The human species, by virtue of its extraordinary brain, has survived enormous environmental challenges over millions of years, the ravages of plague and disease, and the destruction and death caused by countless wars. Along the way we have produced Socrates, Leonardo, Shakespeare, Beethoven, Jefferson, Dostoyevsky, and Einstein. Now we have also produced the instruments of our own destruction, and we are moving toward that destruction with unerring single-mindedness.

"I have concluded that we have a simple choice: we can either give up—just accept that our brains include among their remarkable capacities a fatal flaw that destines us to self-destruct—or we can find a new way of doing the business of nations, a way of halting what Albert Einstein called our "drift toward unparalleled catastrophe."

"I have no illusions about how easily we can change the path that we are on or about whether I alone can precipitate that change. But I believe that we must try—*someone* must try. So, for the sake of my despairing daughter and all the other young people who have lost hope for the future, I am morally compelled to search for a new and safer path. To that end, I am tonight announcing the first two of what I hope will be a long series of steps away from the abyss of nuclear war.

"First, as all of you know, for almost forty years bitter East-West clashes have been part of the continuing superpower confrontation in Europe. We face each other, massed and poised to strike, with forces thickly arrayed on what the world now knows as the Iron Curtain. Europe, the site of so many major wars, could be the site of the last. It is a microcosm of superpower relations, a nuclear tinderbox waiting to catch fire.

"As of this morning, I have ordered the removal of all of my country's nuclear weapons from the territory of our European allies."

He waited for the whispers to subside before continuing.

"Second, you are all aware that the military competition on this planet is on the verge of moving into space. I am convinced that the security we all seek will not emerge from such a competition. As a consequence, this morning I issued a directive halting all of my nation's work on space weapons. And I am calling on all of the nations of the world to come together in a global effort to conquer the frontier of space—to see if there *are* planets we might someday escape to when our own sun dies and to find out if, in all of the vastness of the cosmos, we are alone. That is a far, far better vision of our future challenge in space than a mindless competition toward yet another arena of weapons competition and destruction.

"As you might guess, many of my advisors are deeply concerned about how dangerous these actions might prove to be. Some have even suggested that my emotional state has made me unfit for the grave responsibilities of my position.

"On the other hand—and this is an argument I used with both our allies and my advisors—these actions cannot be advertised as anything except the merest token. The missiles based in my country and on our submarines can rain death upon the great cities of our adversaries with only a few minutes' notice. All I have done is to remove one of several layers of obscenely redundant destructive power . . . and to halt the development of yet another.

"But even this must be taken as what it is intended to be—a gesture of my own good faith and a challenge to the good faith of all other nations which claim not to want nuclear war.

"If my challenge is responded to in kind, as I fervently hope it will be, both nations will have acknowledged that we have more to fear from the products of combined fear than from one another's intentions.

23

If reciprocal gestures are not made within six months, however, I will be compelled to move my nation's nuclear forces back to their current positions and to continue our development of space weapons.

So, as the leader of my nation, I am delivering this challenge as an ultimatum: If our adversaries will not respond rationally to these actions, we will have to go back to business as usual—and to the inevitable disaster that promises.

"As the father of a daughter who lost her child to despair, I am delivering this challenge as a plea: I beg of you all, let us begin now to seek a way of living together on this planet—living in peace."

At first, the entire congregation in the general assembly hall sat in stunned silence. Then someone rose and began clapping. Others immediately joined in and then, as they say, the place went wild. Ambassadors and officials, journalists, everyone in the place cheering and shouting, embracing, tears streaming down weary faces, suddenly bright with hope.

DON'T CALL US, WE'LL CALL YOU

The head of state and the U.N. ambassador of the other superpower had listened to The Speech, as it would soon come to be called, with noncommittal composure. And before the tumultuous response had died down enough for anyone to notice, they had left the room.

In their capital city, high-level civilian and military officials were known to be meeting almost continuously over the days that followed, struggling to break an apparent deadlock over the proper response to the challenge their government had been presented.

The successive waves of rumors that swept the world became increasingly less optimistic as people in every nation waited for the official announcement . . . and waited.

We'll never really know how long they would have waited or what they would ultimately have heard, for after only three weeks there was another speech, and another surprise.

STEPPIN' OUT

The prime minister of Israel had hinted to the international press about a "major policy speech," but it had been unaccountably delayed amid reports of Israeli officials embarking on mysterious errands to certain capitals.

When the speech was delivered, it was in a kind of bad news/good news format. The prime minister first announced what the world had long suspected: Israel had an arsenal of tactical and intermediate-range nuclear weapons which it was prepared to use "if necessary to ensure our ultimate survival." Before the outcry in the Knesset chamber over that bald statement had quieted, he continued with a second announcement. On behalf of the governments of Israel, France, and the People's Republic of China, he was calling for a Nuclear Summit Conference which would include, as "observers," representatives of those nations that were still considering whether to build nuclear weapons.

Public support of the summit swelled immediately. Unprecedented numbers of calls, letters, and telegrams were logged at both the White House and 10 Downing Street. Within two weeks, all of the nuclear weapons states and twelve "observer" nations had agreed to attend the conference, which was to be held in Hiroshima, Japan, in July of 1986.

And as the ember of hope grew brighter in the world, the challenge put forth in The Speech was finally met—in kind and without posturing.

By June 15, 1985, the only nuclear weapons left in Europe belonged to Great Britain and France.

DON'T LOOK BACK

On August 6, 1986, all eyes turned once more to television, this time to witness a formal ceremony at the Hiroshima Memorial and to hear the results of the long closed-door sessions of what came to be known as the First Nuclear Summit Conference. Reading the communiqué, the mayor of Hiroshima announced that the nuclear powers had committed themselves to "halt forever" the buildup in their respective nuclear arsenals, to declare an immediate moratorium on new nuclear weapons, and to establish inspection and monitoring procedures which would guarantee "full and open access" to the nuclear weapons deployment and production facilities of all the nuclear powers. For their part, the observer nations had agreed not to proceed with any efforts to acquire nuclear weapons, while the existing nuclear powers were pursuing a new goal, that of cutting the planet's arsenal of 50,000 nuclear weapons by "at least two-thirds" by the end of the century.

At the same time, and to many people's surprise, the announcement indicated that the assembled nations saw no hope of ending the threat of nuclear war through a reduction of nuclear arsenals. Instead, they were calling for a second nuclear summit to be held as soon as possible on "the challenge of preventing war in the Nuclear Age."

MAKING EVERY MINUTE COUNT

Looking back, it seems from that point on every time you turned around there was some new meeting or treaty to be announced. The notion of survival through cooperation was beginning to become almost commonplace.

In November of 1986, the Cairo Summit was held to begin consideration of the Palestinian question and regional security in the Middle East.

The Second Nuclear Summit, held as scheduled in San Francisco, produced a unanimous commitment to explore "every mechanism known to humanity" for peaceful resolution of international conflict. As a temporary measure, the pope, the secretary-general of the United Nations, and all living winners of the Nobel peace prize agreed to act as mediators in all existing and future disputes between nation states.

Within weeks, the superpowers announced both an agreement on dramatically increased trade and an ambitious ten-year program of educational, cultural, and scientific exchanges.

In March of 1988, the United States and the Soviet Union met in Leningrad and committed themselves to halt "the competition in weapons of destruction, both nuclear and conventional, which denies our responsibility for the future of our children and all of humanity." Two years later these negotiations produced the Treaty of Leningrad, which halted the U.S.–Soviet military competition in every major weapons category from intercontinental ballistic missiles to destroyers and tanks.

FINGER POPPIN' TIME

And then the instruments of peace started selling like hotcakes.

In 1991, a moratorium on the export of tanks, warplanes, and other major conventional weapons was agreed to by all nations.

In 1993, the Treaty of Jerusalem settled the Palestinian-state issue and established permanent borders for the Israeli state and universal recognition of Israel's right to exist.

In 1995, the global agreement to freeze national borders was intended to "end forever the curse of territorial competition" which had led to so many of the planet's devastating wars.

And then last year, in the 1998 Peace Treaty of Chicago, all of the countries of the world agreed "once and for all, to banish war and the use of force as a means for resolving disputes between nations to our dark and barbarous past where slavery and human sacrifice also once reigned" and to take up a new challenge—a response to the discovery, due to radio signals from a far-off galaxy, that we are not alone.

CELEBRATE

We are now just a few hours away from another global event— the celebration of the new century and a global commitment to what is being called "A Millennium of Peace." In virtually every city, town, and village in the world, midnight, December 31, 1999, will be marked by a children's candle-lighting ceremony and a joyous celebration. In New York, the ceremony will take place in the darkened hall of the United Nations General Assembly, with a gathering of children from every nation in the world. And the first candles will be lighted by a girl and a boy, now seven and ten,

27

whose mother once had no hope for the future and told her father,
who told the world:

>Tell me what you want to do in life;
>Tell me what you'd like to see.
>I threw stones at you one time,
>You threw 'em back at me.
>You've got the power to change it—
>You've got the final word.
>Make it better or make it worse:
>Just speak and you'll be heard.
>
>But have you had a vision?*

*From "Have You Had a Vision?" by Ian Sutherland. © 1973 by Smash Brothers
Music, Ltd. Reprinted by permission.

2

SALVATION ROAD

Why You Are the Best Hope for Preventing Nuclear War

This vision of the world moving gradually toward greater safety over the next fifteen years is not some pie-in-the-sky miracle requiring either divine intervention or the spur of alien spaceships hovering menacingly over Duluth or Kiev to make the international system get its act together. It is a perfectly feasible picture of what *could* happen if the two superpowers—or at least one of them—would take the lead in turning around the cycle of increasing paranoia and danger.

The problem, of course, is that it is these very superpower nations—the United States and the Soviet Union—in their frantic competition for "just enough" nuclear weapons to ensure their respective security, have created the combined arsenals that jeopardize hundreds of millions of lives at this very moment. (Zero to 50,000 nuclear weapons in 38 years is hardly a success story.)

And since we are the ones whose lives are endangered, we—and that includes you—really should be thinking of what we can do to make the vision a reality instead of waiting with our fingers crossed for a world leader to have a personal crisis and to commit a consequent act of courage.

GOING IN CIRCLES

For all the dramatic differences in their systems of government, the democratically elected leaders of the United States and the Communist Party–selected leaders of the Soviet Union have something striking in common: despite nearly four decades of official words of alarm and a growing recognition of how completely a full-scale nuclear war would destroy both nations, neither government has been able to find an alternative to the bizarre game of suicidal leapfrog known as "the arms race."

So the question is: what hope is there that either nation can find a different way of doing business at this late date?

I WONDER WHAT THE KING IS DOING TONIGHT?

When it comes to national security policy, the United States and the Soviet Union have something else in common: they both work a lot like monarchies.

In the Soviet Union, the General Secretary of the Communist Party is ultimately responsible for decisions about foreign and military policy. Of course, he is also ultimately responsible for every other kind of policy, so he relies heavily on the judgment of a set of appointed advisors. These "national security experts" are people whose education and experience have made them pretty savvy about how to ensure the physical security of the Soviet Union against the use of hostile force and about how to pursue its interests around the world.

In the United States, the president is ultimately responsible for decisions about foreign and military policy.* Of course, he is also ultimately responsible for every other kind of policy, so he too relies heavily on the judgment of a set of appointed advisors. These "national security experts" are people whose education and experience have made them pretty savvy about how to ensure the physical security of the United States against the use of hostile force and about how to pursue its interests around the world. Sound familiar?

And if you think that the small communities of American and Soviet national security experts don't think a lot alike, just look at what they've been doing. Both groups believe that carrying a big enough stick to make "the other guys" think twice before attacking is the only way to safeguard their respective security. This strategy is called "deterrence" or, more technically, "deterrence of attack by intimidation." How this strategy got to be so popular (and why it is so unreliable as a long-term solution to the nuclear war problem) is described in Chapter Three.

This situation has led to a sort of intercontinental ballistic PR problem: while the national security experts of both governments are struggling to make sure that their side has a stick that is just as big as—or maybe just a little bigger than—the other's, the people they are supposed to be protecting are feeling less and less safe. And no wonder, when both populations are painfully aware of the nuclear weapons aimed at them by "the other side."

So John Jones and Mary Smith in Topeka are starting to worry about whether their kids will reach adulthood . . . and to wonder whether the king and his advisors in Washington really know

---

*The Constitution specifies that the president is commander in chief of the armed forces. The Constitution also specifies that Congress has the power to declare war, and to raise, maintain, and make rules governing armed forces. "National security policy" as such isn't mentioned at all, but in the 197 years since the Constitution went into effect, Congress has largely left national security matters in the hands of the president.

what they're doing. Presumably, Evgeny Orlov and Nina Ste-
panova in Smolensk are beginning to wonder the same thing
about their king and his court in Moscow.

And that's where the similarities end.

BACK IN THE U.S.S.R.

What Evgeny and Nina can do about their concerns is pretty
limited. If they are among the six percent of Soviet citizens who
are members of the Communist Party, they can hunker down,
hold their tongues, work hard, and hope to rise through the ranks
to positions of some influence. Then they can ask, politely, "Are
you guys *sure* you know what you're doing?"

Alternatively, they can voice their concerns to friends or even
to the general public and thereby make themselves eligible for
open-ended vacations in the Gulag archipelago, compliments of
the state.

PHILADELPHIA FREEDOM

John and Mary have a much larger and more promising range
of options. Indeed, they have all the extraordinary democratic
institutions of the United States available to them.

They can publicly question the wisdom of national security
decision makers. They can bring other concerned people together
to work out more sensible alternatives to our current strategy for
preventing nuclear war. They can try to convert anyone they can
get to listen to their way of thinking. They can work to incorporate their concerns into the election-year debates on national
security issues—and maybe they can get candidates to think hard
for a change about how humanity can best go about saving itself
from the fruits of its own fear.

And if there are enough John Joneses and Mary Smiths working together, they can make the 1984 election a virtual citizens'
debate and referendum on how the United States can assume a
leadership role in turning the world away from nuclear war.

DON'T THINK TWICE, IT'S ALL RIGHT

At this point you're probably wondering why John and Mary have waited until now to start working on the nuclear war problem.

The short answer is that most people would rather think about root canals than about nuclear war.

The horror of it—half the American population dead, all of our major cities destroyed, no modern medical care for the survivors, the systems by which we get our food and water and energy devastated, the end of civilization as we know it—is more than our minds can bear to contemplate.

The complexity of it—how humanity managed to get into this tragic mess, the incomprehensible arguments and equations that national security experts toss around, the overwhelmingly tough riddle of how the global drift toward destruction might be turned around—tends to paralyze the intellects of nonexperts.

For these reasons, "we the people"—who under the U.S. Constitution have the right, the responsibility, and the *power* to select the broad strategies of government policies—have preferred to assume that "the experts" know best. But in a world of 50,000 nuclear weapons and six nuclear weapons states (going on sixteen or maybe sixty), we're no longer sure.

TURN TO STONE

The period of public complacency about nuclear war seems to have started after the Cuban missile crisis in October of 1962. We watched with our hearts in our mouths while the United States and the Soviet Union stood eyeball to eyeball over the deployment of Russian missiles in Cuba. When the Russians backed down and then were willing to sign the Limited Test Ban Treaty within a year, it was as though we had witnessed sure proof that our policymakers had the problem of preventing nuclear war well in hand. With a collective sigh of relief, we put the whole nasty subject out of our minds—and kept it out for nearly two decades.

The national consensus on how to prevent nuclear war was a tacit one: let the "king" and his experts in Washington take care of it, and please, *please,* spare us the details.

BAD MOON RISIN'

The first hard evidence that the national consensus on U.S. nuclear weapons policy was falling apart occurred as the Senate considered ratification of the SALT II treaty in 1979. The alarm over the nature of Soviet troops in Cuba (are they for training or for combat?) and then the Russian invasion of Afghanistan suggested to many senators that they should "check with the folks" before voting on the SALT II Treaty—and the folks said "not so fast." Yet without an arms control agreement, it looked as though the nuclear arms race was going to be an open sprint with no hurdles. People started getting scared.

As a consequence, starting in 1979 and 1980, increasing numbers of Americans decided that they really should try to figure out what this prevention of nuclear war stuff is all about. The resulting debate has, for the most part, concerned specific arms control measures—the Freeze, the Geneva negotiations on long- and intermediate-range nuclear forces—and specific new weapons systems—the M-X, B-1, Pershing II, cruise missiles, etc. Feelings run high on every side of the issue, but the debate has created more heat than light and there is no sign of its leading to a new public consensus on how to prevent nuclear war.

When you think about it a little, you begin to suspect that the debate is not proving fruitful because it's just rehashing the same old concepts. Weapons systems and arms control negotiations are the basic building blocks of the policies that have brought us to our current dilemma. So if "we the people" are going to help improve on what the experts have so far done, we have got to step back and look at a bigger picture. We need to rethink the issue of national security and preventing nuclear war—from the ground up—and with our collective mind open to the possible need for profound changes.

Profound changes? What makes anybody think that this nation, which has historically varied its basic policies only slightly from one presidential administration to another, is capable of profound changes in policy? Continuity is our thing, right?

Yes, Virginia, continuity is our thing, and it basically has served this nation well. But there's at least one example to show that profound change is possible if it's what "we the people" want.

ONCE UPON A TIME IN THE WEST

The cycle of economic disaster that began with the great Wall Street crash of October 1929 changed the tenor of American life profoundly. The results of the dramatic deterioration were everywhere—jobless people, homeless people, people waiting hours in line for soup or day-old bread. Nobody could quite understand what had happened or why, but nobody doubted that the change was real.

When Franklin Delano Roosevelt proposed to the American people, during his first presidential campaign in 1932, that a profoundly changed universe demanded that we at least try some approaches that were alien to any government policies of the past, a majority of the electorate agreed. And although these policies did not abruptly and magically make the Depression go away, Roosevelt stuck with the New Deal and the people elected him three more times. Some Americans complained and some "experts" cursed him for his economic blasphemy, but even more people opted for his leadership and for his courageous vision that might lead to recovery.

The legacy of that vision remains with us today in the expanded range of domestic issues Americans have come to believe are the proper and necessary focus of government policy. What was in the 1930s a "radical" new approach to how the U.S. government might conduct its—our—business has become the electorate-endorsed broad strategy for internal policy. We recognize that it has not done away with every potential economic and social malady, but we can see that it has made the very worst possibilities a lot less likely.

And although succeeding presidential administrations have interpreted Roosevelt's vision in varying ways, none has overtly suggested that we go back to our old way of thinking.

NEVER BE THE SAME

The cycle of events that began with the first test of an atomic weapon at Alamogordo, New Mexico, on July 16, 1945, has also profoundly changed the world in which we live. An increasingly restive American public is beginning to suspect that a correspondingly profound change in our way of thinking is called for, but the impetus is developing slowly.

One reason for this national foot-dragging is that the spectacle of bread lines and homeless families in the Depression has no equivalent in the Nuclear Age. We go about our daily lives—working at our jobs, raising our kids, trying to solve our individual problems—without any constant and dramatic reminders of the cataclysm that could be unleashed after a critical decision is made. We may read and even speak about nuclear war; yet for most of us it remains a comfortably remote abstraction.

But we really can't afford to wait for some "demonstration project" that will make the threat of nuclear war as real to us as, say, inflation or unemployment. A nuclear war today would "merely" eradicate life as we know it; if things go on as they are, a nuclear war twenty years from now could eradicate capital-L Life from this planet.

For the nuclear genie is permanently out of the proverbial bottle. We might destroy every nuclear weapon and reactor, burn all the relevant books, and labotomize all the scientists, but the reality of nuclear weapons and of their unparalleled destructive power will remain a condition of human existence forever—forever! It is part and parcel of our legacy to our children, and they, in turn, will leave their children a world which can in thirty-odd years build the instruments of annihilation.

It looks as though we are going to have to find a way to live with this profound and permanent change in our universe.

WHERE DO WE GO FROM HERE?

So far no American leader has come forward with a promising new overall strategy for preventing nuclear war. What is needed is the kind of breakthrough vision with which Roosevelt responded to the changed universe of the Depression. Nor have we any particular reason to think that any other world leader will provide an inspiring new idea and have the courage to launch it.

So it looks like "we the people" of the one superpower nation with a system guided by the will of its citizens are going to have to work with our elected leaders and "the experts" to find a new approach to preventing nuclear war—one that will take us into the twenty-first century and well beyond.

We—and that includes you—have got the basic equipment to meet this, the most urgent, challenge that any generation of human beings has ever faced: We possess the instinct for survival and what everybody's mother called "enough sense to come in out of the rain."

The only other requirement is a place to start, and that one's easy: We'll begin at the beginning.

3

WHERE DO WE GO WRONG?
How Humanity Got into This Awful Mess

One day several thousand years ago, a caveman named Runt suddenly decided that he'd had just about enough of a caveman named Oaf pushing him around and taking his food. So the next time Oaf came around looking cranky and hungry, Runt picked up a rock and yelled, "If you hit me, you're gonna be sorry!"

Well, lo and behold, it worked. Oaf was so astonished that he just stood there with his mouth open and then turned around and walked away.

Thus was born the strategy called "deterrence of attack by intimidation." Everybody in that whole tribe of cavemen thought it was a terrific idea. In fact, after thinking about it awhile Oaf decided this was such a great idea that he came around the next day with an even bigger rock and shouted "Mess with me, pipsqueak, and you'll regret it for sure."

And so it went. Before long, the whole tribe had taken to carrying around rocks to make the other tribes leave them alone. Of course, the other tribes took all this rock-carrying stuff as a threat and started carrying around even bigger rocks to ensure *their* safety.

AND THE BEAT GOES ON

As the tribes moved, in turn, to bigger and bigger rocks, it became clear that the next biggest size would soon be too big to pick up, much less convince someone you could throw, so somebody invented a catapult. As human culture became more sophisticated, people moved on to spears, then longbows and crossbows.

When somebody invented gun powder, deterrence by intimidation got a whole new lease on life from muskets, cannons, rifles, light artillery, heavy artillery, bombs, etc. The spurs of fear and mistrust kept people developing bigger and bigger "rocks."

Throughout all this time, deterrence by intimidation proved itself again and again to be a sound strategy—the best strategy—for personal, tribal, and national security. Countries even had specially trained people called "national security experts" who figured out how to make bigger rocks than the ones their enemies had and what to say to make sure everyone knew they were serious about not being messed with.

Of course, sometimes deterrence failed and countries got into wars . . . but there was usually someone left to tell about it.

(GOODNESS GRACIOUS) GREAT BALLS O' FIRE

In 1938, the United States government received intelligence reports that Germany was working on a new weapon which used

The dot in the center square represents all of the firepower used in World War II, including the atomic bombs dropped on Hiroshima and Nagasaki. The 6,000 dots in the rest of the squares represent the comparative destructive power of the nuclear weapons that exist today. Just two squares on the chart represent enough firepower to destroy all of the large- and medium-sized cities of the world.

the power released by splitting atoms. Knowing that our entry into World War II was inevitable, we secretly started to develop a rock that would be as big as, or bigger than, whatever the Germans might come up with.

By the end of the war, Germany had failed to develop the new weapon, but the United States had demonstrated to a startled world the previously unimaginable destructive power of the atomic bomb on human populations and the cities in which they live.

In the aftermath of World War II, the uneasy alliance of the capitalist United States and the communist Soviet Union quickly fell apart, and the Cold War began. Mindful of the power that the now-hostile Americans possessed as the sole owner of atomic weapons, the Soviets tested their own "rock" in 1949.

In the thirty-five years since then, each superpower struggled ceaselessly to make sure that its pile of rocks was bigger than its adversary's.

And this is what that competition—deterrence by intimidation in the Nuclear Age—has provided.

Moreover, these weapons are controlled by machines and human beings—sometimes in that order. Neither are infallible.

PANDORA'S GOLDEN HEEBIE JEEBIES

RUPERT: Damn it! I told you I didn't want to know about this stuff. Now I won't get any sleep tonight, and I've got to work on an ad campaign tomorrow.

CLARITY: You mean you're scared? Are you beginning to wonder whether deterrence by intimidation can be expected to work forever?

RUPERT: I'm beginning to wonder whether deterrence by intimidation is going to work till the end of the week. But why are you making me listen to this? What can I do? And so what if you're right about the democracy stuff—that "we the people" do have the power to participate. How can ordinary people decide what *kinds* of changes might work? The guys with the fancy educations—U.S. *and* Soviet—haven't been able to find an alternative to deterrence by intimidation. How can John Jones and Mary Smith and Rupert Vanderkopf hope to do any better?

CLARITY: It has something to do with not seeing the forest for the trees . . . and spending too much time counting each other's leaves. Let's get started.

4

STARTING ALL OVER AGAIN

A Commonsense Approach
to Finding a Way Out

CLARITY: O.K., Rupert, rev up your common sense. In the face of the increasing global threat of nuclear war, what is your goal?

RUPERT: That's pretty obvious. My goal is to make sure that I and my kids and their kids don't get wiped out by nuclear weapons—to make us all safer.

CLARITY: Good. Then what is the problem we have to solve?

RUPERT: Equally obvious. The problem is stopping the nuclear arms race.

CLARITY: Wrong. The nuclear arms race could be brought to a screeching halt tomorrow and you might not be one iota safer. Stopping the nuclear arms race will not prevent nuclear war; it's going to take a lot more than that. Think about the big picture and try again. What is the problem?

RUPERT: Well, I guess the problem is preventing nuclear war.

CLARITY: Excellent. Now how do you go about figuring out how to prevent nuclear war?

RUPERT (AFTER ABOUT FOUR MINUTES OF SILENCE): I don't know. It's too scary and too complicated for me to think about.

CLARITY: O.K., let's practice on something that's a little less complicated and a lot less scary. Suppose you were planning to plant tomatoes in your backyard next spring and the problem was making sure that your tomato crop wouldn't get wiped out. How would you figure out what to do about that?

RUPERT: Well, I guess I'd start by making a list of all the ways that my tomato plants could get wiped out: insects, diseases, not enough water or light, not enough nutrients in the soil. Then I'd think of all the things I could use to make sure that none of these tomato tragedies actually would happen. You know, choosing strong varieties of plants and a good plot with water nearby, preparing the soil thoroughly, laying in some fertilizers—that kind of thing.

CLARITY: Terrific. Now how would you apply the same process to solving the problem of preventing nuclear war?

RUPERT (AFTER ONLY TWO MINUTES OF SILENCE): Well, if you work on both of these problems the same way, I guess I'd start by making a list of all the ways that nuclear war could begin. Then I'd look at each item on the list and try to think of all the things that I could do to make sure that it doesn't happen.

CLARITY: You're getting pretty good at this commonsense business. Let's see how it works.

PRESERVATION ACT ONE

There are six basic once-upon-a-future-time story lines for the beginning of a nuclear war. National security experts, who have been thinking about such things for a long time, call them "doomsday scenarios." For us nonexperts, it's probably more useful to think of them as six "fuses" on a bomb—six different fuses that could set off a full-scale nuclear war.

Fuse #1:
YOU BEAT ME TO THE PUNCH

The first scenario is called "a bolt from the blue." It's what would happen if one of the superpowers suddenly decided that it was sick and tired of being jerked around by the other one and opted to settle things once and for all with a sudden, unprovoked, and massive nuclear attack. The primary objective of such an attack would be to wipe out all of the weapons with which the other nation might retaliate.

To date, most nuclear arms control negotiations between the United States and the Soviet Union have been intended to make it inconceivable that either side would rationally decide launching "a bolt from the blue" is a good idea. The concept at work in this matter is called "mutual assured destruction" or MAD. It basically assures that each nation will survive a first strike with enough mobile (as in bomber or submarine-launched) and well-protected (that's what all the talk about "hardening" missile silos is about) nuclear weapons intact to inflict "unacceptable damage" in a retaliatory strike.

Essentially, the U.S. and the U.S.S.R. have worked cooperatively to maintain this "balance of terror." Both governments recognize that as long as they can credibly say to one another, "If you hit me, you are absolutely, positively going to be hit back almost as hard," neither side will make a rational decision to launch a preemptive attack. Now as to whether we can be sure that the leaders of both sides will remain rational under crisis conditions . . .

Fuse #2:
IT'S ALL DOWN TO GOODNIGHT VIENNA

A second way that nuclear war might begin is through escalation in a European crisis. The United States and its NATO allies and the Soviet Union and its Warsaw Pact allies have massive military forces deployed on either side of the Iron Curtain. In the face of the numerical superiority of Warsaw Pact troops, the NATO nations have stated that if they were unable to turn back an attack with conventional forces, they would resort to the use of so-called "tactical" nuclear weapons. We've got 5,000 in Western Europe right now. Since the Soviet Union also has lots of tactical nuclear weapons, what happens after the first one is used by either side is uncertain—except to most Europeans. They think it would be the last European war for a long time.

Fuse #3:
ROCK THE CASBAH

Most national security experts think that under current conditions the most *likely* way nuclear war would start is through escalation of a Third World crisis. Although there are some Third World "hot spots" that don't involve the United States and the Soviet Union—the ongoing war between Iran and Iraq is an example—there are many more in which the superpowers are providing military and economic aid and political support to opposing sides. Some of these exist in the Middle East, Central America, and Northeast Africa.

Although the superpowers are ever-mindful of the possibility of one of these confrontations leading to full-scale nuclear war, it is all too easy to think of ways this could happen. We almost came to blows with the Soviets in the 1973 Middle East war as we both resupplied our clients. And it's going to be a lot more scary when some of the countries in these hot spots get nuclear weapons of their own.

Fuse #4:
BLINDED BY THE LIGHT

How about nuclear war because of technical failure? Both the United States and the Soviet Union have complex and tricky electronic systems—manned by complex and tricky human beings—to warn them of a pending nuclear attack. The history of interesting malfunctions in these systems makes it all too possible that a full-scale nuclear war could be started because of a false alarm.

In November 1979, the main computer at the headquarters of the North American Air Defense Command in Colorado Springs broke down. In accordance with an established contingency plan, a backup computer was activated immediately. What wasn't in the contingency plan is that someone had left a "war game" practice tape in the backup system. For several minutes, until the error was discovered, the Soviet Union was thought to have launched land- and submarine-based ballistic missiles at the United States. Shudder.

Fuse #5:
JUMPIN' JACK FLASH

The growth in the global arsenal of nuclear weapons and in the number of nuclear reactors around the world makes it increasingly likely that a terrorist group will at some point either steal a nuclear weapon or get its hands on enough weapons-grade fissionable material to manufacture a crude bomb.

Now just suppose that one day, during a period of the "usual" tension between the superpowers, a square mile or so of Manhattan is suddenly vaporized by a nuclear explosion. If U.S. detection systems have not indicated an incoming weapon, how would our decision makers react? Would they feel compelled to act quickly against the "most likely" source?

We'd prefer not to find out.

Fuse #6:
IT'S A MISTAKE

Both of the superpowers are concerned about and have instituted elaborate measures to prevent the unauthorized or accidental use of nuclear weapons. In the United States, the chain of command includes numerous safeguards, and the actual launching of a weapon requires the participation of several people and the unlocking of an electronic safety mechanism with a numerical code.

The effort to prevent the kinds of episodes portrayed in *Dr. Strangelove* or *Fail-Safe* is serious indeed, presumably as much in the Soviet Union as in the United States. As we all know, however, both people and electronics can malfunction.

Just suppose that a mechanical failure accidentally launches a Pershing missile from a site in West Germany to a target in the Soviet Union. With good communications, we might be able to let the Soviets know what had happened before the missile hit, but

49

not in time for evacuation. Faced with the destruction of one of their major communications centers in western Russia, would the Russians believe our claim of an accident or would they suspect a ruse—perhaps an attempt to disable their communications network in preparation for an all-out attack?

Once again, we'd prefer not to know.

PRESERVATION ACT TWO

Given these six "fuses" by which nuclear war might start, what can we do to make sure that they will not be ignited in the first place or that they will be snuffed out before they burn all the way?

If you examine the six fuses to nuclear war, you can see right away that deterrence of attack by intimidation, the cornerstone of both superpowers' strategies for preventing nuclear war, should continue to work in preventing a "bolt from the blue" preemptive attack. With absolute certainty that its adversary will be able to inflict "unacceptable damage"—say, wipe out two hundred major cities—in a retaliatory strike, neither the United States nor the Soviet Union will ever make a cool and rational decision to launch a preemptive attack.

Unfortunately, the other five doomsday scenarios don't involve the kinds of circumstances in which we can be sure that coolness and reason will prevail. In a rapidly deteriorating European or Third World crisis, high level decision makers may not have time to consider the ultimate ramifications of each stage of escalation as they react to quick changes in conditions. Similarly, in the confusion that would follow a false alarm or the kind of single nuclear explosion that would result from terrorism or the accidental launching of a weapon, the people in charge must make split-second decisions: Do those blips on the radar screen mean what we think they mean and should we therefore launch our own missiles before the silos are hit? Do we have time to figure out who vaporized Manhattan and whether they did it on purpose, or should we launch our own weapons before what might be the rest of theirs get here?

Under such stressful circumstances, human beings have been known to make less than totally rational decisions. In other words, deterrence by intimidation—the "balance of terror" assured through arms control agreements—is simply not adequate to prevent nuclear war under five of the six doomsday scenarios.

ANTICIPATION

What this nation needs, then, is a *more comprehensive* strategy for preventing nuclear war, one that takes into consideration *all* of the "fuses" that could set off a full-scale holocaust. And we can fairly easily figure out what the critical additional elements in a comprehensive strategy would be from the doomsday scenarios themselves.

If we want to make sure nuclear war doesn't start from a major East-West confrontation in Europe, then we should look to lowering the overall level of hostility that exists between the United States and its allies and the Soviet Union and its allies.

To make sure the end of the world doesn't start in a Third World crisis, we should try to keep nuclear weapons out of the hands of Third World governments and look to what we might do to help such countries, indeed all countries, resolve their disputes without resorting to military force. And just in case they still end up in wars, we should try to limit the scale of those wars by stemming the enormous tide of state-of-the-art conventional weapons to those regions—which is going to take a great deal of cooperation between East and West.

The ultimate key to preventing a nuclear war from starting over a false alarm lies also in making a substantial improvement in the overall relations between the United States and the Soviet Union, for it is during periods of extreme tension that decision makers are most prone to mistakenly jump to the conclusion that those blips on the radar screen really are incoming enemy missiles.

The obvious means of preventing nuclear war from beginning after a terrorist's nuclear detonation is to keep nuclear devices out of the hands of terrorists. This clearly involves keeping nuclear weapons from spreading to any nation that supports terrorism or that might not be too careful about securing its nuclear weapons, but it also requires much tighter international controls on the fissionable materials from which a primitive bomb could be manufactured. And while these long-term measures are being implemented, it would also help a lot if our relations with

51

the Russians weren't so dismal that we would automatically assume a nuclear explosion in Manhattan was caused by a Soviet weapon.

Better U.S.–Soviet relations could also keep a nuclear war from occurring if, in spite of every precaution, a weapon from one side or the other was launched accidentally or without authorization. It is equally critical, however, to have instant and accurate means of communication between Moscow and Washington. If a message like, "I don't know exactly how to tell you this, but a couple of our people just went berserk and in about twenty minutes something pretty awful is going to happen to Omaha (or Vladivostok)" didn't get through in time or wasn't believed, it could result in hundreds of millions of deaths at both ends of the transmission lines.

I CAN SEE FOR MILES

When you sort these elements out, the list of "firebreaks" in the path to nuclear war looks like this:

FIREBREAK #1: Improving Overall U.S.–Soviet Relations
FIREBREAK #2: Nuclear Arms Control
FIREBREAK #3: Nuclear Nonproliferation (preventing the spread of nuclear weapons to nations that don't now have them)
FIREBREAK #4: Reducing International Traffic in Conventional Arms
FIREBREAK #5: Improved Crisis Communications Mechanisms
FIREBREAK #6: Peaceful Resolution of International Conflict

The first firebreak on the list is, as you probably already suspect, the most immediately important. The obvious point is that the superpowers, armed to a fare-thee-well and spitting at one another like tomcats, constitute the most likely current threat of full-scale nuclear war. Beyond that, however, the state of overall U.S.–Soviet relations is a *major* determinant of how well the other five firebreaks can work.

With our having 10,000 nuclear weapons targeted on the Soviet

Union and their having a like number aimed at us, the necessity of taking on the U.S.–Soviet relationship as a problem to be solved is evident—and formidable. But then, nobody ever said democracy would be easy.

If improving U.S.–Soviet relations is the "most important" and the toughest firebreak in the short term, it is the last one on the list that is the key to preventing nuclear war in the long term—and probably the most challenging. Yet, peaceful settlement of international disputes may be an idea whose time has finally come.

The father of modern physics, Albert Einstein, recognized this possibility very early. In November of 1945, before anyone had shown how $E = mc^2$ could make light bulbs glow, he wrote in the *Atlantic Monthly:*

> Since I do not foresee that atomic energy is to be a great boom for a long time, I have to say that for the present it is a menace. Perhaps it is well that it should be. It may intimidate the human race into bringing order into its international affairs, which without the pressure of fear it would not do.

Thirty-odd years later, we lesser intellects are finally beginning to suspect that making sure Einstein's "may" becomes a "will" is humanity's most urgent business.

So let's get on with it.

BREAK ON THROUGH

Most of the "firebreak" problems are tough ones with unpromising histories and no easy-as-pie, "right" options for the future. And at the implementation stage, some of them are extremely complicated—which is why we really do need national security experts.

What is important to remember is that your proper role in the national security triumvirate of electorate/president/experts is to weigh the selection of the approach that our government should adopt for solving each of the firebreaks problems. You don't have to be an expert to exercise this right and responsibility of your citizenship: you only have to understand the basic functioning of each firebreak.

Think about it this way: Do you have to be an expert on soil texture to understand how digging a broad ditch in the path of a forest fire will keep the conflagration from spreading?

Each of the firebreaks works in a way your common sense will easily grasp. In the chapters that follow we explain how they function and suggest some fruitful ways that you—and the people who want to be your elected "agents" for establishing a national security policy—can think about them. We believe you'll end up drawing some pretty sound conclusions about which policy options are the most promising components of a broad strategy for preventing nuclear war.

And we've tried to help you along by suggesting some specific issues for you and the people who want to represent your interests in forging a national security policy to think about. These are presented in the form of questions interspersed in the six "firebreaks" chapters.

Those headed "Listen to What the Man Says" are questions that any serious candidate for the presidency should be compelled to answer concretely so that "we the people" can understand how he or she plans to prevent nuclear war. We can then plan accordingly.

Those headed "Think for Yourself" are intended to stimulate your commonsense, vested-interest thinking about long-term solutions to the problem of preventing nuclear war and to present some options that might not otherwise occur to you.

5

WHY CAN'T WE LIVE TOGETHER?

Firebreak #1:
Improving Overall U.S.–Soviet Relations

CLARITY: Want a little perspective on the Russians? Try this. Imagine yourself narrowly escaping from a sinking ship in the middle of the night and hundreds of miles from any known land mass. As the sun rises, you realize that drowning may be the least of your problems, for the water turns out to be swarming with five-megaton sharks. They don't seem too interested in you so far, but snack time is bound to come before long.

Suddenly—miracle of miracles—you spy a tiny but green island only a few hundred yards away. This prospect of safety is like a shot of adrenaline and you start swimming rapidly toward it.

As you approach the island, however, you make a horrible discovery: It is already occupied by an obnoxious fellow passenger from your ship—a fellow who has proven himself to be defensive to the point of paranoia and who is bullying, abrasive, self-righteous, arrogant, and prone to violence.

Your choices are painfully clear: you can either opt for certain death and dismemberment in the jaws of the sharks or face the prospect of spending the rest of your life on a tiny island with a real creep.

What would you do?

RUPERT: I know what you're getting at, but the analogy is ridiculous.

CLARITY: The analogy is only ridiculous if you think the Nuclear Age strategy of deterrence by intimidation is going to work *forever*. This planet *is* a tiny island; we don't have anywhere else to go—or to suggest the Soviets go—for the present. Civilized coexistence with the other most powerful resident is obviously going to be difficult and frustrating, but the longer we stay in the water with the gathering sharks, the more perilous our lives become.

RUPERT: I still don't see how buddying up to the Russians, even if it were possible, is going to prevent nuclear war.

CLARITY: Nobody's talking about buddying up to anyone. Look, try it this way. Name a country across the ocean whose government follows economic principles alien to our own and whose international behavior often runs counter to our wishes. It withdrew abruptly from a military alliance with the United States and has a nuclear arsenal that could devastate every major U.S. metropolitan area.

Give up? It's France. Now, how worried are we about getting into a nuclear war with the French?

RUPERT: Nobody ever worries about a nuclear war with France. The whole idea is crazy. It simply wouldn't happen.

CLARITY: Why are you so sure?

RUPERT: We just don't ever get that mad at the French. We may find them cranky and uncooperative on occasion and they may find us a little on the arrogant side, but basically we've learned to get along.

CLARITY: Eureka! The magic formula. We're trying to get along
. . . and learn about each other.

HENCE, IT DON'T MAKE SENSE

The ongoing hostility between the United States and the Soviet
Union is a little like the legendary feud between the Hatfields and
the McCoys; hardly anyone remembers why it started and there
are even several conflicting versions of how. But that doesn't
seem to matter much. Our cycle of international sniping and
jockeying has developed a momentum of its own.

CLARITY: Think about it. Is there any particular reason why
this planet shouldn't be big enough to accommodate one self-
declared "superpower" that is politically democratic and economically capitalist and another self-declared "superpower" that
is politically authoritarian and economically communist?

CHUCK: But wait a minute. I think it's time I contributed to this
discussion. In case you've forgotten, it's the Russians who think
this planet is too small for both communism and anything that
isn't communism. Don't they still worship Lenin, who once said
that "the existence of the Soviet republic side by side with the
imperialist states for a long time is unthinkable"?

And it's easy to see that they have held on to the Marxist dream
of taking over the world—and not letting go of a thing. Didn't
they invade Afghanistan because the *communist* leader wasn't
tough enough on rebels? Haven't they gone into Hungary and
Czechoslovakia with Russian troops when those governments
wouldn't lean hard enough on their own people? And I'll bet they
threatened to do the same thing in Poland when that Walesa guy
was making them nervous.

Haven't they tried to buy or muscle their way into countries all
over the world, either directly or through their surrogates, by
aiding revolutionaries and guerrillas in Asia, Africa, and Central
America?

And who precipitated what came damned near to nuclear war
by trying to put missiles in Cuba—right on our doorstep—in
1962? And who knows what they were planning for Grenada?

And why do you think the Soviets have built all those missiles?
Who do you think those 10,000 warheads are targeted on—

Australia? If we didn't scramble to keep up we'd be finished. The 10,000 nuclear weapons we have aimed down their throats are the only things that are keeping the Russians from swallowing up this whole planet!

VANYA: Hah! Just listen to him. Now do you see why we need our nuclear arsenal? It's the only way we can survive in a world that would like nothing better than for the Soviet Union to disappear.

The United States and its World War I allies were happy to see us overthrow the tsar in 1917—that is until they discovered the Russian people did not want another bourgeoisie-dominated "democracy" that would continue to provide cannon fodder to the Germans. Do you know that in 1918, before the Bolshevik government could even establish domestic order, the Allies, recruiting the Japanese to help them in the East, sent thousands of troops to Russia and thereby succeeded in prolonging our national unrest? Should we have seen this as a joyous welcome to the international system?

The United States gets all worked up about our helping Castro in Cuba but are we not supposed to be worried about their military presence in places like Turkey, which is right on our borders? They have allies in our hemisphere. By what planetary rule can we not have allies in theirs?

When the United States, which claims to love democracy, has been willing to support repressive regimes in South Africa, the Philippines, Greece, Iran, and throughout Central and South America as long as they were "anti-Communist," are we supposed to think that Americans are seriously interested in peaceful coexistence? Or democracy, for that matter?

When we are called an "evil empire," are we supposed to take it as an overture of friendship? We know those 10,000 U.S. warheads are not aimed at China.

Our nuclear arsenal is the only thing that keeps the Americans from getting rid of us once and for all!

CLARITY: This is really exciting—Tweedle Dum and Tweedle Dee on the slippery slope to nuclear war.

WHY CAN'T YOU BEHAVE?

Whatever the complex roots of our conflict with the Soviet Union, foremost in the minds of American policymakers and the

American people is the Russians' international misbehavior: exacerbating Third World conflicts, invading Afghanistan, demanding that Eastern European governments toe the Party line and squelch dissent, shooting down that South Korean commercial airliner, and sending Cubans to fight in countries like Angola and to undermine countries like Grenada. How can we deal with such people?

Well, how do we go about deciding how to deal with children—or adults—who continually misbehave? We usually start by trying to figure out what's wrong with them or what they're up to.

There are two major schools of thought on what the Soviet Union is up to and why it maintains such an enormous military establishment.

Those Soviet experts who see the Russians as out to take over the world by hook or by crook cite Marxist-Leninist ideology, with its emphasis on the global incompatibility of communism and capitalism, the inevitability of conflict, and the goal of Marxist universalism, as well as the tsarist Russian affinity for territorial expansion.

Those experts who think that the Soviet Union's actions can best be explained by an insecurity that borders on paranoia make their arguments based on Russian history. They cite the enormous losses Russia suffered in invasions from Western Europe during the Napoleonic Wars, World War I, and World War II; the deep-seated Russian "inferiority complex" that dates from the late seventeenth century; and the chronic social and economic problems that leave the Soviet Republic with little but military muscle to flex in asserting its superpower status. Many also assume that the inherent defensiveness of the Soviet leadership is magnified by the fact that the United States, Great Britain, France, and the People's Republic of China have all or the vast majority of their strategic nuclear weapons targeted on the Soviet Union.

Think for Yourself. Do you think that the Soviet leadership operates with a Russian-dominated Communist Earth as a high-priority day-to-day, year-to-year goal? Or do you think that, like the United States, the Soviet Union often ends up giving lip service to ideological dreams, maybe even wishing they might come true, but acting pragmatically?

Listen to What the Man Says. Any close examination of Soviet behavior inevitably indicates that, whatever else they may be up to, the Russians do suffer from a high degree of insecurity about both their national safety and the world's view of them as a major power. So do we. Pay attention to how the candidates answer the following questions:

- Do you think Soviet international behavior is motivated more by insecurity or aggressiveness?

- Do you believe that the Soviet Union has any legitimate reasons for its belief that we would like to put them out of business permanently?

- What can the Soviet Union and the United States do or say to reassure one another that they see no alternative to peaceful coexistence in a world of tens of thousands of nuclear weapons?

- Do you believe the U.S.–Soviet Third World competition for hearts and minds (and occasionally military bases) is likely to go on for the foreseeable future, and if so, shouldn't we be trying to make that competition less dangerous before one of these Third World playing fields turns into the first battleground of World War III?

WE DON'T TALK ANYMORE

The United States and the Soviet Union have at least one acknowledged common interest: staying out of nuclear war. Each understands that such conflict would be devastating to both; each insists that its nuclear weapons are required only to keep the other nation from acting on its worst impulses.

So you'd think we'd have a lot to talk about and a strong mutual interest in keeping the conversation going.

The fact of the matter is that the president of the United States and the general secretary of the Soviet Union have only met *once* in the past eight years. And the second most powerful official in each country on nuclear war issues—the U.S. secretary of defense and his Soviet counterpart—have met once in the whole 38 years of the Nuclear Age. Our secretaries of state and arms control negotiators meet, but they rarely have anything to show for it. Scientific, cultural, and educational exchanges have been reduced to less than half the level of the late 1970s. Opportunities for U.S. and Soviet citizens to meet privately are virtually nonexistent.

So how do we, in fact, communicate on what are ultimately life and death issues? As publicly as possible. Off (occasionally) and on (mostly) for the past 38 years, the U.S. and Soviet heads of state and their subordinates take turns making ringing speeches and delivering thundering statements to the press about each other and the relationship of these two countries.

The substance of these "communications" is almost entirely ritualistic: threat and counterthreat, scolding and counterscolding, epithet and counterepithet, all interlarded with declarations that their respective governments are dedicated to peace. These exchanges keep the satellite links, the telex lines, and the type setters at *Pravda* and the *New York Times* very busy, but they could hardly be called a dialogue.

VANYA: Of course we don't talk. The United States government won't agree to face-to-face meetings on any level until we set up all domestic and foreign policies exactly the way they want them.

CHUCK: Ha! The reason we can never get together is that the Russians are afraid everyone they let out of the country will make a run for freedom!

CLARITY: Okay, guys, let's face it. One reason leaders on both sides are reluctant to meet is that they are afraid to come out and tell the reporters that (Horrors!) they haven't produced any dramatic new agreements to sign. It's a kind of theater where the play can't start until all kinds of major pending business has been negotiated so that they can go in, sit down, sign their John Hancocks and Karl Marx's, and come out all smiles, looking like they've made wonderful breakthroughs. They're apparently afraid that they will be tarred and feathered if they don't come home with the Magna Carta or something.

GET CLOSER

Many experts think that the Soviet Union and the U.S. will never defuse their relationship unless the *people* in the two countries "get closer." There is clearly no way to begin this rapprochement without a serious commitment by the decision makers on both sides—the people and elected officials in the U.S. and the communist hierarchy in the Soviet Union.

If we decide to undertake such an effort, the first step would be to open new doors to tourists and exchange students, as has happened with the U.S. and China. This step is a particular challenge to the Soviets, with their penchant for secrecy and their closed society, but Americans have traveled and studied in the Soviet Union.

A major challenge to us is the language. There are currently more teachers of English in the Soviet Union than there are students of Russian in the United States. This will have to change if we are going to effect the kind of changed relationship we have attained with the Chinese.

Listen to What the Man Says. Regularly scheduled meetings between U.S. and Soviet heads of state and cabinet-level officials and a commitment to expanded people-to-people programs could improve relations in good times and minimize deterioration during periods of tension. Pay attention to the candidates' answers to:

- How frequently should summit meetings and other high level conferences be held?

- Should they be conditional on "good" behavior? Should we each give the other a global deportment grade before we agree to meet?

- Can cultural and educational exchanges help further understanding between the Soviet people and the American people? Would expanding such exchanges to include the arts and popular entertainment like films and television programs be useful in this regard?

- Should the government support expanded programs in Russian language education?

TRAGEDY

On September 1, 1983, Soviet fighters intercepted and shot down a (South) Korean Air Lines 747 that had strayed into Soviet airspace near sensitive military installations.

A great many questions remain to be answered about this incident. How did the KAL plane wander so far off course? Why was it allowed to stray into Soviet airspace for well over two hours without having been contacted so that its course could be corrected by the international civil aviation system? Did the Soviets recognize it as a civilian jet? How hard did they try to warn it off or force it to land before they shot it down?

Whatever the answers to these questions, the fact remains that 269 lives were lost, and virtually the whole world was appalled.

Some lessons to be learned from this tragedy are:

1). Whether the decision to shoot the plane down was made in Moscow or by a regional military commander acting in accordance with rigid standing orders, it is clear that the Soviets judged the possibility of military secrecy being breached to be more important than either humanitarian concerns or international repercussions. The priorities built into the Soviet system are very different from ours, and if they change at all, it will be very slowly.

The United States and the rest of the world must deal with the Soviet Union and the Russians as they are, not as we wish they were. We must put together as detailed a portrait as we can of their values, their own perceptions of their interests, and of their idiosyncrasies; and we must deal with them pragmatically.

2). We must work into this portrait of the Soviet Union the fact that various Soviet objectives may conflict. In recent years Moscow has worked hard, both domestically and internationally, to portray the Soviet government as strong and not to be trifled with, but essentially committed to peace. What has been universally greeted as an act of paranoid barbarism has been a major setback to this campaign, perhaps on both fronts.

3). The current level of tense mutual suspicion between the United States, with its allies, and the Soviet Bloc can all too easily turn minor-league human errors into international tragedies. The loss of life in the KAL incident was measured in the hundreds. What would have happened if the flight had been Pan Am 007 and everyone lost had been an American? Conscious decision or blunder, in another context such an incident could lead to the loss of far more than just the 269 people who died in the Sea of Japan.

Listen to What the Man Says. The KAL incident is bound to come up during the election campaign. Listen to what individual candidates have to say about making sure that this tragic bit of history isn't repeated.

- What kinds of U.S. policies can effectively modify Soviet behavior?

- Would arrangements for more direct and immediate communications between East and West help prevent such incidents?

- Shouldn't the U.S. and the Soviet Union reach agreement on "rules of the road" in the air just as we have at sea, including better means of communication between airplanes?

STAYIN' ALIVE

The first decision that the U.S. government, and thus the American people, must make about how to deal with the Soviet Union involves selecting an overall approach of either "disengagement" or "engagement."

Think of rival teenage gangs who want to avoid a murderous rumble and go after that goal by yelling at each other across the street, putting various preconditions on whether their representatives can meet to divide up the local turf, and bad-mouthing each other to the rest of the neighborhood. That is disengagement.

It is the approach we used with the Soviets during the Cold War period, and we seem to have reverted to it since the beginning of 1980. It involves keeping them at arms' length, engaging in ritualistic communications geared as much to the world audience as to the Soviets, letting everyone know how strongly we deplore their human rights practices and international behavior, and slapping them on the wrist in ways that embarrass them even when we suspect that it won't get them to change their ways.

Engagement is the way we describe a commitment to talking and dealing with the Soviets on as many fronts as possible in spite of their misdeeds. The best example of engagement to date took place in the period from the late 1960s through the late 1970s. We both called the effort "détente," a French word for the relaxation of tensions.

The accomplishments of détente under the Nixon, Ford, and Carter administrations were significant. In 1972, the SALT I agreement limited antiballistic missile systems, ICBMs, and submarine-launched ballistic missiles. The Helsinki Agreement, signed by President Ford in 1975, covered prior notification of military maneuvers, exchanges of observers, increased cultural and scientific cooperation, and the promotion of human rights.

President Carter continued the détente policy of his predecessors, pressing forward on the SALT II talks which produced an agreement in 1979 and pursuing negotiations on reductions of NATO and Warsaw Pact forces in Central Europe, a comprehensive ban on nuclear weapons testing, and limitations on conventional arms exports. For a while it was really looking as though the superpowers had begun to work seriously on their common major problem—preventing nuclear war.

ANOTHER ONE BITES THE DUST

But détente collapsed, each side blaming the other, of course, although a review of pertinent events suggests that both countries contributed to the deterioration of their relations.

The 1972 Jackson-Vanik Amendment to the East-West trade bill tied the granting to the Soviet Union of most-favored-nation status, which reduces import tariffs, to liberalization of Soviet emigration polices. The Soviets howled and backed out of the East-West Trade Agreement, one which some officials from both governments had estimated would have tripled the volume of trade between the superpowers.

Then, in early 1973, the Soviets started testing their new family of ICBMs. In one case, they trotted out a bigger-than-expected missile, proving, among other things, that they had outmaneuvered Nixon and Kissinger in the eleventh hour of the 1972 SALT I negotiations. We screamed foul and they told us to go reexamine the treaty's language.

In 1976 the Soviets sent Cuban troops to Angola. We objected vigorously to this intervention—especially when their side won.

In 1977, President Carter's human rights campaign, together with a call from the Western European Communist Parties for liberal democratic rights and less harsh treatment of Soviet dissidents, again got Moscow worked up on what it considered interference in "internal" Russian matters.

In 1979, after the SALT II Treaty was signed, things looked better. Then two months later we found a Soviet "combat brigade" in Cuba and declared the situation "unacceptable." They said we were nuts, that it was a training brigade, and that it had been there since the sixties. (Mayor Frank Rizzo of Philadelphia wondered out loud what all the excitement was about and offered to send a contingent of Philly cops down there to clean out whatever Russians there were.)

Then in late 1979, the Soviet Union invaded Afghanistan. President Carter took the lead in organizing an international boycott of the Moscow Olympics. He curtailed grain exports and Soviet fishing privileges, suspended cultural and scientific exchanges, and restricted exports of high technology and other strategic materials. He also called for the Senate to hold back on consideration of the pending SALT II agreement.

Since early 1980, then, relations between the United States and the Soviet Union have basically been Cold War Revisited.

This sequence of events points to some tough decisions the American people must face in determining how they will deal with the Soviets in the future.

Think for Yourself. It is clear that the U.S.–Soviet relationship went from the engagement of détente to the current disengagement largely because of a disagreement between the two sides on what constitutes acceptable behavior outside the context of agreements. Both moral and practical questions are involved.

The first question is: Since the goal of improving U.S.–Soviet relations, testified to by every president from Truman to Reagan, is not friendship per se but rather a substantial reduction in the threat of full-scale nuclear war, can the greater moral good be achieved by cooling the relationship through hitting each other hard and publicly on "unacceptable" policies or by swallowing our "revulsions" at each other's behavior and keeping the communications links open?

The follow-up question is a practical one. Both sides are supersensitive to criticism. Each sees in public rebukes that the other has assumed the role of a holier-than-thou adult who is chastising a juvenile delinquent in front of the whole gang. Yet how can we balance wanting to let the world know what our respective moral and practical standards are without making each other more intractable? Which consideration is more important to the overall goal of preventing nuclear war?

The major *practical* question about engagement and disengagement is best understood by going through a simple exercise. In evaluating the overall effect of any U.S. response to Soviet misbehavior, or vice versa, you have to ask the following four questions about each statement or sanction:

1). How does it affect the other side? Whether or not it "hurts" them in some way, does it successfully change their behavior?

2). What is its domestic economic effect?

3). How does it affect relations with our allies and other members of the world community?

4). How does it affect the overall U.S.–Soviet relationship and therefore the threat or prevention of nuclear war?

Using these questions, what decision would you have made with respect to tying trade to emigration policies? About the grain embargo and Olympics boycott following the Soviet invasion of Afghanistan? About the suspension of scientific and cultural exchanges after this invasion? About the suspension of Aeroflot landing rights after the KAL incident?

6

BACK OFF BOOGALOO

Firebreak #2:
Nuclear Arms Control

RUPERT: May I be excused from this session and still get my picture in the book? I don't think I can deal with nuclear arms control.

CLARITY: Why ever not?

RUPERT: Well, I have this condition that's sort of like an allergy. Whenever I hear words like "Euro-strategic balance" and "telemetry encryption," my eyes glaze over and this muscle in my neck contracts convulsively, forcing my head into the ground. It's really quite painful.

CLARITY: I think we can cover this subject without using any language that might have such an unpleasant effect on you.

Let's go back to Runt and Oaf, or maybe their great-grandchildren. By this time human culture was far enough along to have gotten into theology, and two tribes, the Titans and the Colossi, had been fighting for eons about whether the "real" god was the Sun God or the Rain God. At some point it might have occurred to everybody that each tribe could just worship whatever god it preferred, but by that time the tribespeople had been hurling insults and decayed fruit at each other for so long that they just couldn't stop.

So all the adult males in each tribe were walking around with rocks in their hands all the time and yelling, "We wouldn't need these if we could trust you, you creeps!" at the other tribe. As they started carrying bigger and bigger rocks, however, it finally occurred to both tribes that if they really got into a full-scale rock fight, it could be curtains for everybody. The Titans and the Colossi could all end up bashed and bleeding and dead; this would be a war with no winners.

What a dilemma! They didn't trust each other enough to just agree to put all the rocks down, but the ongoing struggle by each side to make sure that it had the biggest rocks was getting really dangerous—to say nothing of the hernia epidemic it was causing.

So the Colossi said to the Titans, "Look, this is getting ridiculous. We both have these things that we don't want to throw and don't want thrown at us, but we're afraid to put them down. What if we just try to make sure that we both have exactly the same number of rocks? That way, neither of us will be tempted to start a rock fight because we'll know for sure that you'll throw as many at us as we can throw at you and kids will be killed and we'll both be very sorry it ever happened. If we know we will both suffer 'unacceptable damage' no matter who starts the rock fight, neither of us will start one. Neat, huh?"

The Titans agreed that it was a good idea, and after some discussion it was decided that each tribe would be allowed fifty rocks, plus a live-in observer from the opposite side to make sure neither tribe secretly stockpiled rocks.

But wait a minute. What if the Titans had 50 middle-size rocks and the Colossi had fifty big rocks? You might figure that was about even because the middle-size rocks could be thrown further than the big rocks, so the Titans could theoretically strike from a site out of the range of the Colossi's really big rocks. On the other hand, if the Colossi managed to launch a sneak attack with their big rocks, they could wipe out the Titans in no time.

Since the Colossi had been worrying about the Titans having big rocks as well, the two tribes successfully negotiated a new agreement: 50 rocks of no more than eight pounds each and, again, the live-in observers.

But then the Colossi noticed that the Titans seemed to be rather tall, with arms in proportion to their height. The Titans must not have felt taller than the Colossi, for when the Colossi suggested negotiations on the size of the people allowed to throw rocks, they agreed. The result was: fifty rocks of no more than eight pounds each to be carried only by people who were five feet eight inches or shorter—and a live-in observer.

But then one day it occurred to the Titans that the size of the people allowed to carry the rocks around wouldn't matter very much if those people had catapults. What a great idea! The problem was that no Titans knew how to make catapults or how long that would take to figure out. What if the Colossi had the same idea, and they made a catapult first? An absolutely destabilizing discovery and the proper subject for further negotiations.

Fortunately, the Colossi weren't sure how to make a catapult either; so an agreement was reached to permanently outlaw catapult technology, and both tribes had one thing less to worry about.

And they just kept on that way, agreeing not to let people carrying rocks climb hills or hide behind bushes, not to allow rocks with sharp edges, and not to allow marble rocks (which were exceptionally hard). They just wanted to keep things relatively cool.

RUPERT: That doesn't make any sense.

CLARITY: What do you mean, it doesn't make any sense? It's very simple. As long as the Colossi knew that even if they struck first the Titans would be able to retaliate with "unacceptable damage," and vice versa, everybody felt pretty confident that ongoing squabbles could be limited to exchanges of insults and rotten fruit, both of which were unpleasant, but not lethal. As long as nobody did anything irrational, it was a pretty stable situation.

RUPERT: I understand that part. What I don't understand is why, if these guys could sit down and agree on all these rules, they just couldn't just agree to put down their rocks altogether.

CLARITY: You've got to remember that these guys were cavemen—not very high up the evolutionary scale. You know, a bit thin in the neocortex.

And humanity has really made quite a lot of progress in the past few thousand years. I mean, we aren't negotiating about *rocks* anymore, are we?

GET ON THE GOOD FOOT

As indicated above, the first point to understand about nuclear arms control efforts is that their primary objective is stability—ensuring a stable "balance of terror" so that neither side is tempted to attack the other because of a perceived advantage.

The second important point about nuclear arms control agreements between the United States and the Soviet Union is that, short of their leading eventually to total nuclear disarmament, which is not currently even much of a gleam in anyone's eye, *they cannot prevent nuclear war.* Even an across-the-board nuclear freeze negotiated tomorrow might not prevent a full-scale nuclear war next week if the superpowers get into a major confrontation.

Indeed, recent history suggests that success in the cooperative control of our nuclear arsenals is more likely to be the *effect* than the cause of improved U.S.–Soviet relations. During the period of détente, some U.S. officials had high hopes that the SALT negotiations could be the sturdy workhorse that would pull the cumbersome cart of U.S.–Soviet relations out of the diplomatic Stone Age. What happened, of course, is that the deterioration of relations eventually scuttled the negotiations, particularly the effort to have the SALT II agreement ratified by the Senate. In retrospect, it looks as though progress may best be made by modernizing the cart and loading the disappointingly frail horse inside.

SUSPICIOUS MINDS

Given the state of U.S.–Soviet relations for most of the past 38 years, it's not surprising that the overall achievements of negotiated arms control have been so inadequate. After all, we wouldn't be having to make rules about what we can have in our respective arsenals if relations between the superpowers were anywhere near civil.

And the mistrust that fuels the arms race is reflected at the negotiation table in radically different assessments of the status quo (the U.S. went into the current talks on limiting nuclear weapons in Europe claiming that the Soviets had a six to one advantage; the Russians said the European arsenals were about even), hostility, posturing for the benefit of a larger audience, and a good deal of gratuitous mutual jerking around.

VANYA: Jerking around is an understatement. The United States mouths pious platitudes about commitment to nuclear arms control but uses every excuse to obstruct progress. You didn't like our dealings with Czechoslovakia in 1968, so you delayed the beginning of the SALT I negotiations which *you* had proposed in the first place.

SALT II would have been a comedy of errors if the subject hadn't been so important. First we negotiated with your people in good faith, getting close to an agreement, and then you came in and said, "Sorry. We've had a change of presidents and we're going to have to change our positions." Then, after the treaty was signed with hugs and smiles all around, you said, "Sorry, we don't like what you did in Afghanistan and we won't ratify the treaty." But we *are* committed to arms control and have abided by the provisions of the treaty in the hope that you will eventually come to your senses.

And in other talks you open with absurd demands—which is O.K., everybody does that. But you stick stubbornly with yours for months and months, making us look like monkeys for even trying to deal with you in good faith.

CHUCK: Who tries to make monkeys out of whom? There are worse things than sticking with a position—like not sticking with it. It wasn't *our* head of state who waltzed into one of the final negotiating sessions of SALT I and basically said, "You guys can quit dotting those *i*s and crossing those *t*s now, cause we've changed our minds on a major part of the agreement."

GOOD NEWS

The existence of 50,000 nuclear weapons in the world today is eloquent testimony to the paltry progress of human efforts at nuclear arms control. But the news is not all bad.

What is most heartening is that the United States and the Soviet Union, which not only control the lion's share—ninety-five—percent of those 50,000 weapons but have most of that destructive power aimed at each other, have remained willing, if often gracelessly so, to keep plugging away at nuclear arms control, even while their overall relations are going to hell in the proverbial handbasket. Their somewhat cranky tenacity in this undertaking tells the world what we all badly need to know: that behind all the rhetorical excess and posturing, both governments understand the danger of staying too long in the water with the sharks—sharks they themselves have created.

Some of the notable successes of U.S.–Soviet nuclear arms control negotiations have been those that limited whole categories of weapons competition. The results are that nuclear weapons tests in the atmosphere, under water, and in outer space are banned; nuclear weapons may not be deployed on the seabed, in earth orbit, or in outer space; Antarctica is off limits for any nuclear weapons testing or deployment. Similar measures have severely restricted the size of and circumstances under which underground nuclear weapons tests may be conducted and have effectively prevented a senseless U.S.–Soviet competition in antiballistic missile (ABM) systems.

POWER TO THE PEOPLE

Here is a bit of information that should put some wind in your sails as you approach the challenge of "working" on the nuclear war problem through the 1984 elections: Public opinion has been and continues to be an important factor in our government's decisions to pursue nuclear arms control.

World concern about the hazardous effects of radiation from above-ground weapons testing in the late 1950s led to the Limited Test Ban Treaty (LTBT) of 1963. That the United States and the Soviet Union were willing to negotiate on nuclear testing within a year after the Cuban missile crisis is evidence of the impetus that the public's sense of urgency can give to arms control efforts.

Success with the LTBT created a public appetite for broader arms control measures in the United States and this led to the Salt I negotiations.

The original SALT talks proved exceedingly difficult, but they ultimately produced an agreement limiting antiballistic missile systems and a modest start at controlling offensive nuclear weapons. Members of the Senate, who invariably "see what the folks are thinking" before voting on critical issues, ratified the two agreements by a vote of eighty-eight to two.

More recently, widespread public support for a bilateral nuclear weapons freeze has had a substantial impact on the national arms control debate.

Negative public opinion in the United States has, on occasion, slowed arms control negotiations. Outrage at the Soviet invasion of Czechoslavakia in 1968 led President Johnson to delay the start of SALT I, and a similar reaction to the invasion of Afghanistan in 1979 contributed to the Senate's suspension of the treaty ratification process.

JUST DROPPED IN (TO SEE WHAT CONDITION MY CONDITION IS IN)

Once you understand that the primary goal of nuclear arms control agreements between the United States and the Soviet Union is to maintain stability by maintaining the "balance of terror," you can begin to see why so many people get excited about the question that's most often posed in the corrupt and meaningless form "Who's Number One?"

What's really at issue is whether or not there's a rough balance between the overall capacity of the U.S. and Soviet nuclear arsenals. If they *are* balanced, then we can safely negotiate for balanced limitation or reduction of nuclear weapons. If the Soviet arsenal is significantly superior, then we should either build up our own to match it before engaging in negotiations or negotiate for limitation or reduction ratios that will create balance. Simple, huh?

From here on in it gets a little complicated.

First of all, there are currently two separate questions of balance at issue in conjunction with two separate negotiations.

1). Are the two strategic arsenals, i.e., U.S. long-range weapons that can reach the Soviet Union and Soviet long-range weapons that can reach the United States, roughly balanced?

2). Are the two European nuclear arsenals, i.e., U.S. and NATO weapons that can reach the Soviet Union from Western Europe and Soviet weapons that can reach Western Europe, roughly balanced?

Second, you can count any of several weapons numerically: launchers (missiles and bombers), warheads (many weapons now have several warheads that can all be aimed at separate targets), or total arsenal yield in megatons (one megaton equals the explosive power of one million tons of TNT). Moreover, the numbers themselves must be modified by such considerations as the reliability and accuracy of various weapons systems and their vulnerability to destruction before they reach their targets.

As you probably suspect by now, what you count and how you weigh the qualitative factors determines whether you conclude that they're ahead, we're ahead, or we're about even. Radically different conclusions about whether balance exists are likely to be as big an issue in the 1984 presidential campaign as they are at the negotiating tables of Geneva.

> **Think for Yourself.** However complicated this "bean counting" stuff may sound, nonexperts can master the basics, and in "When You're Hot, You're Hot" we've suggested some sources of information designed for interested citizens. But even without detailed knowledge of the specific numbers involved, there are some important things you should think about when listening to what presidential candidates have to say about their ideas on nuclear weapons and arms control.

> • How likely is it that either the Soviet Union or the United States will bide its time while the *other* superpower builds up its arsenal to what *it* considers parity?

A 1983 article in *Time* magazine pointed out a basic truth of the nuclear arms race:

> One superpower's margin of safety is the other's sense of being inferior and threatened. There can be no such thing as

a one-sided buildup. One way or another, there will be competition. The only question is whether the competition will be ameliorated and regulated by arms control.

• Since the stability sought in negotiated arms control agreements is reciprocal deterrence by intimidation, how much is enough? When the Soviets know that just one surviving U.S. Poseidon submarine could destroy 160 Soviet cities, how likely is it that they would ever make a rational decision to launch a first strike? When the Americans know that if only three percent of the Soviet land-based missiles survive a first strike, they could destroy 165 American cities, how likely is it that we'll ever make a rational decision to strike first? Within the context of these kinds of figures, how important is it that the "balance" equation be worked out to the last detail?

• Can we trust the Russians? This question has come up in regard to the unratified-but-committed-to SALT II agreement; the proposed bilateral freeze on the testing, production, and deployment of nuclear weapons; and the current negotiations in Geneva. The answer is that the question is irrelevant.

If we trusted the Soviets and they trusted us, we wouldn't be in this mess in the first place. Nuclear arms control agreements are not handshakes between friends. United States negotiators simply do not sign any provisions that cannot be checked out reliably by our spy satellites and other sophisticated means of intelligence collection. Listen to What the Man Says. We are not trying to downplay the complications of nuclear arms control decisions, but if you listen carefully to the candidates' answers to some basic questions and the follow-up questions they get from the press or, in a debate, from their fellow candidates, you will be able to make some basic judgments on how sound their reasoning is.

> • Do you think that a rough balance exists between the U.S. and Soviet arsenals in Europe, or do you think we have to deploy more weapons before we can expect the Soviets to negotiate seriously?

> • How should the nuclear arsenals of China, France, and Great Britain be limited in arms control negotiations? In

light of our relations with these countries, what might the United States do to encourage their participation in arms control efforts?

- Do you think it is a good idea that every American nuclear arms control proposal be one that advances Soviet security interests as well as American ones?

7

WHO'LL BE THE NEXT IN LINE?

Firebreak #3:
Nuclear Nonproliferation

The critical role of nuclear nonproliferation—keeping nuclear weapons from spreading to nations that don't already have them—in the prevention of nuclear war is obvious. The more countries that have nuclear weapons, the more likely it is that such weapons will actually be used, especially by nations facing disastrous defeats in conventional wars.

PLAY WITH FIRE

CLARITY: To get an idea of the state of nuclear nonproliferation efforts in the world today, imagine a group of fierce tribes living uneasily together on a dry and windy island.

A few powerful and advanced tribes had gained control of the island's entire flint supply and so were able to make fires to cook their food and heat their huts. But one of these tribes also figured out that flint had weapons applications and soon developed special arrows that could be set on fire before they were shot to burn down enemy villages. Alarmed at this new threat to their security, the other tribes with access to flint hastened to build fire-arrow arsenals of their own.

There was only one little problem with this great new weapons system: none of the tribes was sure that the whole island wouldn't catch fire if the fire arrows were ever used in battle. So there they were, saddled with mighty weapons that they couldn't risk using. None of the tribes in the Fire Arrow Club wanted to be the first to cast their weapons into the sea, and since they couldn't work out how to do it simultaneously, they just kept them. And even though having the things around was rather nerve-wracking, each of the tribes kept making more, so that their enemies would know that they weren't to be messed with.

Meanwhile, the less advanced tribes on the island had developed a yen for cooked food and warm huts, and they began clamoring for flint from the Fire Arrow Club tribes.

The club members faced a difficult dilemma. The prospect of trading flint for other materials—and forming helpful alliances in the process—was extremely attractive. On the other hand, some of the tribes who were requesting flint were pretty wild—just the kind of guys who would have the island incinerated in no time if they ever got their hands on fire arrows.

After mulling it over, the club members concluded that since fire arrows were a bit tricky to make anyway, it was safe to provide flint to any tribe that would swear on the spirits of their revered ancestors never to make fire arrows—and would submit to occasional inspections. Under the Fire Arrow Nonproliferation Treaty, which codified the arrangement, the club members also pledged to work cooperatively toward the goal of casting their own fire arrows into the sea, over time.

All the parties to the treaty understood that a fire arrow-free island wouldn't necessarily be a peaceful island, but the risk of it's ever being consumed by fire would be minimized. It looked like things were under control.

Fifteen years after the treaty was signed, the picture was a lot grimmer. Rather than getting rid of their dangerous weapons, the Fire Arrow Club member tribes had more than trebled the size of their arsenals. Consequently, some of the tribes that were supposed to be using flint only for peaceful purposes decided they'd be safer with a few fire arrows of their own; with the advances in technology, they just weren't that difficult to make. In fact, any tribe with a bit of flint and a "burning" desire for fire arrows could find a way to whip up a few.

And that is essentially what has happened with nuclear weapons.

RUPERT: But nuclear weapons have got to be harder to make than some arrow that you set on fire!

CLARITY: They're a lot harder to make. The nuclear material needed to manufacture a weapon can be obtained from the fuel used in a research reactor or separated out from the spent fuel of a power reactor, but the processes involved are tricky, expensive, and difficult to undertake in secret.

Nonetheless, when the Nuclear Nonproliferation Treaty was signed in 1968, the only Nuclear Club members were the United States, the Soviet Union, Great Britain, France, and China. Fifteen years later, its membership includes India and, in all probability, Israel and South Africa. And this growth has occurred despite the inspections of nuclear facilities and the other safeguards mandated by the treaty and by most bilateral sales agreements for nuclear technology and materials.

At least one nation has dramatically demonstrated how little faith it has in the international system's ability to limit club membership. In June of 1981, Israeli jets flew over Jordan and Saudi Arabia to bomb and destroy Iraq's Osirik nuclear reactor. There were no apologies, just a straightforward explanation: Israeli intelligence had reported that the reactor was intended to build a bomb and that the bomb was intended for Tel Aviv.

LIFE IN THE FAST LANE

Unless the international system for preventing proliferation of nuclear weapons is strengthened considerably, as many as fifteen additional nations could have nuclear weapons by the end of the century.

This does not mean that nuclear arsenals as sophisticated as those of the United States and the Soviet Union could spring up all over the world. It does mean, however, that virtually any country with a power reactor could manufacture a primitive nuclear device, load it into a modified DC-6 or 707, and have a decent chance of detonating it in enemy territory—and that might be enough to start World War III.

The nations that currently seem most interested in acquiring nuclear weapons—Iraq, Libya, Pakistan, Argentina, Brazil, Taiwan, and South Korea—are all involved in open conflict with neighboring states or more subtle struggles for regional supremacy.

You will note that several of these nations are what is known as "nontraditional states"; they have histories of government instability or of making the kinds of flamboyantly nationalistic gestures the rest of the world finds unsettling. Others appear less interested in specific targets than in the bizarre international prestige that comes with Nuclear Club membership.

TAKIN' CARE OF BUSINESS

There is obviously very little that any nation can do unilaterally to stem the tide of global nuclear proliferation. Given its international influence and superpower status, however, the United States could move to lessen the short-term problem in a number of different ways. Possibilities include:

• Assuming a stronger leadership role in tightening international nonproliferation mechanisms—the Nonproliferation Treaty, which expires in 1995, and the International Atomic Energy Agency—and urging the participation of nations not yet involved.
• Moving aggressively toward the formation of a nuclear technology and materials suppliers' cartel that would impose the strictest controls on the use, replication, security, and transfer of nuclear fuels and technology.
• Pursuing more actively the substance of the Nonproliferation Treaty, which pledges the United States, the Soviet Union, and Great Britain to "achieve at the earliest possible date the cessation of the arms race and to undertake effective measures in the direction of nuclear disarmament." Needless to say, the superpowers aren't quite holding up their end of *that* bargain.

Until the superpowers and other nuclear weapons states involve themselves more productively in nuclear arms control
efforts, they clearly lack the moral authority of chastise or levy
sanctions against those states which have refused to sign the
treaty or taken shameless advantage of its loopholes.

There is also a practical link between Nuclear Club arms
control foot-dragging and nuclear proliferation. Many of the
nations actively seeking nuclear weapons capacity are simply
afraid of what the club or some of its members might do.
Cooperative efforts to limit or reduce existing nuclear arsenals—
at least to start moving toward a fire arrow-free island—would
encourage non-nuclear weapons states to exercise restraint, both
by example and by lessening motivation.

Listen to What the Man Says. To most Americans, nuclear
nonproliferation is less immediate and frightening than the superpower impasse, but it is a problem which must be addressed now
if we are to avoid disaster through the end of the century. The
candidates should have answers to the following questions:

- What should the United States do to encourage France,
  China, and Israel—all members of the Nuclear Club—to
  sign the Nuclear Nonproliferation Treaty?

- What might the United States do to encourage nations
  such as Taiwan, Argentina, and Brazil—all appear to be
  aiming for nuclear weapons capacity—to sign the treaty?

- Do you think that nuclear proliferation can be halted
  without halting the sale of nuclear reactors and associated
  equipment to Third World Nations?

8

THE THINGS WE DO FOR LOVE

Firebreak #4:
Reducing International Traffic in Conventional Arms

CLARITY: O.K., Rupert, we're going to have a pop quiz on the material covered so far. The multiple choice question is: Which of the six "doomsday scenarios" do national security experts think is the most likely route to full-scale nuclear war under current conditions?

RUPERT: That one's almost too easy. Rock the Casbah—escalation of a Third World crisis.

CLARITY: Right. Now comes the essay question, which is going to require using your head just a bit. How can reducing international traffic in *conventional* weapons help prevent nuclear war?

RUPERT: Well, I guess it has to do with escalation—little wars turning into big wars. Certainly if countries have only primitive weapons to go at each other with—say, spears and machetes—their wars have to remain fairly small-scale one-on-one kinds of things. But when you've got bombers and fighters, even if they're "only" armed with conventional weapons, you can have a pretty bang-up big war. And the next level of escalation, I guess, is nuclear weapons.

I suppose that what it boils down to is that people in the United States and the Soviet Union, as well as people in heavily armed "hot spot" regions, would be a lot better off if the countries that wage wars had to do so without sophisticated modern weapons.

CLARITY: That's a sound explanation of the escalation danger, but it's not the whole story.

If you look at who instigates wars in various parts of the world, it's pretty clear that in some cases the wars are almost frivolous and might not have been started *at all* if the governments involved didn't have high-tech military toys to play with. For instance, Libya's Colonel el-Qaddafi would probably think twice about his adventurism all over northwest Africa if his troops had to do their invading in Piper Cubs and dump trucks. And there's at least some speculation that Argentina's invasion of the Falkland Islands was planned mainly to divert the Argentine population's attention away from that country's chronic economic problems. The quest for glory might have been less tempting if the Argentine army had to make its landing in fishing trawlers.

RUPERT: Still, you've got to hand it to Argentina for chutzpah. They had Great Britain shipping military equipment to them as late as eight days before their grab for the Falklands. Cute, huh?

CLARITY: Well, at least it makes a nice parable about the dangers of arms mongering.

BIG HUNK O' LOVE

The opposing forces in some of the most volatile regions of the world—the Middle East, the Persian Gulf, and Central America—are armed with weapons bought or received as military aid from the more technologically advanced nations. And international arms sales are big business.

- In constant 1979 dollars, worldwide arms exports went from just over ten billion dollars in 1970 to an estimated total of over thirty-five billion dollars in 1983.

- Arms imports by developing countries in the 1961–79 period amount to more than one hundred twenty-two billion dollars.

- The United States and the Soviet Union are the "sellers" in fifty-eight percent of current arms sales and the figure gets a lot bigger when you include the other nations in their respective alliances. *NATO and the Warsaw Pact account for ninety percent of all conventional arms exports.*

BROTHER LOVE'S TRAVELLING SALVATION SHOW

There are at least four major reasons why technologically advanced nations engage in large-scale conventional arms sales.

- Many nations that greatly expanded their arms exports in the 1970s did so in part to correct the enormous balance of payments deficits they incurred when the price of imported oil skyrocketed.

- For the United States and the Soviet Union in particular, arms sales are often part of a package of aid (or trade) and political support on which the return is needed resources and/or opportunities to establish strategically important overseas military bases. The United States developed such a relationship with Iran under the Shah. The Soviet Union had enjoyed access to strategically useful locales as part of its relationships with Cuba, Syria, and Algeria.

- Even when there are no immediately tangible benefits to be gained, the United States and the Soviet Union often provide requested weaponry to win the "hearts and minds" of Third World countries. (The greater U.S. ability to provide economic as well as military aid often serves us well in this "influence race" with the Russians. As one Nigerian official observed, "You can't eat bullets.")

- As weapons have become more sophisticated, the cost of maintaining a modern military force has jumped tremendously. Foreign military sales help defray research and development costs and the fixed costs of manufacturing. A 1979 Congressional Budget Office study estimated that the Pentagon's procurement costs are reduced by fifteen percent and its R&D costs by eight percent through military exports.

There are two more reasons why advanced nations are tempted to sell weapons to Third World countries. Ironically, one school of thought sees conventional arms sales as a means to *reduce* the threat of nuclear war. This idea, called "the dove's dilemma," asserts that supplying nations whose neighbors are hostile with enough weapons to establish a credible deterrent lessens their motivation to develop, by hook or by crook, nuclear arsenals.

And, of course, the answer of last resort to questions about the ethics of international arms sales and the implications for nuclear war is a shrug. "If we don't sell them what they want, somebody else will."

BOOGIE WOOGIE BUGLE BOY

It is clear that reducing the threat of nuclear war by reducing the flow of conventional arms to international "hot spots" requires a high degree of cooperation among arms exporting nations. But the United States is well positioned to attempt establishment of such cooperation. Our links with the NATO countries and with Israel are obvious, and during the latter period of U.S.–Soviet détente, the superpowers actually sat down together to talk about limiting arms exports! Although the Conventional Arms Transfer (CAT) talks failed to produce an agreement, at least they demonstrated that both sides are interested in solving the problem.

Listen to What the Man Says. International arms sales is not a topic that presidential candidates are likely to bring up on their own, but they should be asked the following questions:

- Do you think the U.S.–Soviet competition in supplying sophisticated weaponry to "client" states contributes to the instability of Third World hot spots?

- If elected, will you take some initiative to obtain international agreements restricting the sale of conventional arms to Third World hot spots?

- Specifically, what can be done to involve the Soviet Union in cooperative efforts to solve this problem? Should the United States seek to reopen the CAT talks?

- Should the United States work with our allies to stem the flow of weapons to the Third World? What kind of approach would be most effective?

9

CALL ME!

Firebreak #5:
Improved Crisis Communications

CLARITY: Hey, Rupert. Remember the Cuban Missile Crisis—Kennedy and Khrushchev eyeball to eyeball in the Caribbean? That was pretty scary for both sides, and one of the lessons learned from that episode was that communications between the White House and the Kremlin were dangerously inadequate for handling emergencies.

RUPERT: But don't we have some kind of hot line now?

CLARITY: Yes, a Moscow-Washington Hot Line was established back in 1963 and modernized to incorporate satellite links—one Russian and one American—in 1971. Now, what do you think the hot line actually is?

RUPERT: Everybody knows that: it's a red telephone on the president's desk, with extensions in his limousine and on Air Force One and a similar system in Moscow. And it's not a party line.

CLARITY: Well, you're right about it's being confidential, but it's not a direct telephone. One reason is the language problem. Another is that human beings speaking directly to one another in the middle of a crisis are apt to lose their cool. The misinterpretation of something like "O.K., Yuri, that's it. We're sick and tired of being jerked around by you turkeys. You've had it!" might have extremely grave consequences.

RUPERT: Well, it's still disappointing that there is no red telephone for dramatic midnight conversations. If it's not a phone, what is it?

CLARITY: Nothing that would look very sexy in the movies. It's a two-way teletype that requires translators and operators at both ends.

And it's slow, especially when a ballistic missile launched from a submarine can get to Moscow or Washington in 15 minutes. Clearly we are in a situation where eleventh hour communications that could avert a nuclear war might well arrive long after midnight—when it will be too late. We've got to find a better way for these guys at the top to talk with each other.

Fortunately, it appears that both the U.S. and the Soviet Union recognize the shortcomings in the current system, and are trying to do something about it. Proposals now pending call for: 1) modernizing the hot line, 2) improving communications between Washington and the U.S. embassy in Moscow and between Moscow and the Soviet embassy in Washington, and 3) establishing a communications link between the U.S. Defense Department and the Soviet Defense Ministry.

In addition, the Senate of the United States has proposed superpower negotiations aimed at the establishment of an elaborate new nuclear crisis prevention system. If fully implemented, this system would operate through crisis communications centers—one in Washington and one in Moscow—staffed by both U.S. and Soviet officials.

The general mission of these communications centers would be to monitor and exchange information, through facsimile transmission, voice relay, and even teleconferencing, on any events that might lead to a nuclear incident. Routine functioning of these centers and their personnel might include:

- Establishing procedures to be followed in the event of the unexplained detonation of a nuclear device, terrorist threats to explode a nuclear weapon, discovery that a nuclear weapon is missing, etc.

- Explaining in advance any military activities that might otherwise arouse fear and suspicion in times of exceptional tension.

- Exchanging information—in an atmosphere of professionalism rather than one of political brinksmanship—on nuclear doctrines, forces, and activities with an eye to avoiding any destabilizing surprises.

- Maintaining a data base on the strategic forces of both nations that can be used in negotiating strategic arms control agreements.

HEY, WESTERN UNION MAN

It is easy to anticipate how the smooth functioning of these crisis communications centers in periods of relatively routine superpower relations could build mutual confidence and thus minimize the probability that mischances would lead to disaster in times of exceptional tension.

You can even imagine the Washington center handling a communication from the Soviet Union that would go something like this: "Say, your friends the Soviet Koreans seem to be having another problem with their navigation system. One of their civilian airplanes has been in our airspace for about 20 minutes now and our folks on the Kamchatka Peninsula are getting sort of nervous. Do you think you could get KAL back on course before we handle them 'by the manual'?"

Listen to What the Man Says. The need for improved communications to prevent crises and manage them optimally if they do occur is broadly recognized, but their ideas vary as to how elaborate a scheme is desirable and the breadth of the mission that should be undertaken. Each candidate should be able to state specifically what he would be aiming for in terms of overall scheme, technology to be included, and scope of responsibilities. Listen for the answers to:

- Do you think it's a good idea for a president-elect to go through a thorough training exercise in crises communication problems and procedures?

- Do you support the idea of establishing a joint U.S.-U.S.S.R. crisis communication center that would be staffed at all times by representatives of the two countries?

- Are you in favor of establishing regular contact and communication between the senior military officials of the two superpowers?

- Do you think that advanced telecommunications techniques can be used to improve direct communications between the superpowers? Do you think there are potential dangers in the use of such technology?

10

BRIDGE OVER TROUBLED WATER

Firebreak #6:
Peaceful Resolution of International Conflict

CLARITY: O.K., we've gotten to the point of figuring the "bottom line" for this business of preventing nuclear war, and I'm going to let you do it.

RUPERT: But you're the one who keeps saying there are no easy answers. It's hardly fair to try to make me, a lifelong and deeply committed ostrich who had to be carried kicking and screaming into confrontation with this issue, do the toughest part.

CLARITY: I admit that I thought you were pretty hopeless at first, but you've really done remarkably well. I've got a lot of confidence in your common sense. Just answer a couple of questions and think a little. This one really *will* be easy. Start with this: Given what you've learned in our discussions, what do you think the chances are that nuclear weapons can be made to go away permanently?

RUPERT: Well, I'd like to think that it is at least theoretically possible, but if we're going to be hard-headed about this, I'd have to say that we'll have them around for a long, long time—as far in the future as any of us can see. And I buy the argument that says humans will never be more than 38 years away from 50,000 of the things if someone decides they've *got* to have them.

CLARITY: Sad but true. Now, under current conditions, what is the most likely route by which these weapons would come to be used?

RUPERT: Through escalation—little wars becoming big wars.

CLARITY: So then what do we have to do to keep nuclear weapons from being used?

RUPERT: We have to not have little wa— Wait a minute! I see what you're trying to do. You want me to say, "tra-la-la, all we have to do to prevent full-scale nuclear war is not have wars anymore." Which leads me to believe that no one ever taught you the difference between an ostrich and a turkey. You may think I'm some kind of a birdbrain, but I've spent a lot of time watching *homo sapiens* operate and I am positive that "no war" isn't in the cards for your species.

CLARITY: I didn't say that the answer would be easy to *implement,* just that it would be easy to figure out. And so it was; you got it right the first time. But let me change the words around a little. With the introduction of nuclear weapons, the stakes have become too high for nations to keep settling their disputes by going to war. How's that?

RUPERT: Well, it makes *sense* when you put it that way, but I still don't see it happening. You humans have been talking about controlling war since the dawn of time, and look where it's got you: You're on the verge of incinerating this whole planet.

CLARITY: But that's my point: it is because the survival of the species is at stake that we have an incentive to do what we haven't managed to do before. Anyway, I do recognize that wishing won't make it happen. People didn't just say, "Let's go to the moon" and have Neil Armstrong take off on gossamer wings. We've got to look at what we've got that can get us started in the right direction, then take it on as a kind of developing technology . . . and hope that we're not starting too late.

War is an unusually nasty version of what mathematicians call "a zero-sum game," which means that if one side wins, the other loses. Even on those rare occasions when a war ends in a "negotiated peace," it's typically because one side saw that it was sure to get creamed no matter what and decided to minimize its losses.

The alternative to zero-sum games as a means of settling disputes is a negotiated settlement in which each side compromises as little as possible but both sides "win" on the points that are most important to them.

Here's a homely and nonlife or -death example.

When Susan and Lois each discovered that the other was planning a European vacation, they decided it would be a good idea if they went somewhere together. They'd both save money by sharing a hotel room and a rented car and they'd have each other for company.

When they got down to specifics, however, they quickly reached an impasse. Susan was looking forward to a luxury hotel in Paris in June, and Lois had her heart set on something cheap but clean in Sicily in October. Still, neither of them was that thrilled at the prospect of traveling alone, so they decided to discuss what each of them wanted in greater detail.

It turned out that Susan's yen for Paris in June was based on her enthusiasm for sightseeing, her dread of bad weather, and a fantasy about twelve-foot ceilings and Old World grandeur. Lois had opted for Sicily in October because she wanted to spend at least part of her vacation lolling on a beach without "thundering crowds of tourists" around and because her budget was tight.

Once each of them understood what was really important to the other, they were able to come up with a variety of options that came close to matching both their wishes.

They ended up on the southern coast of Spain for two weeks in August. Their hotel, a small but charming conversion of an eighteenth-century Spanish nobleman's country house, was moderately priced and only a twenty-minute drive from an uncrowded beach. From that headquarters they were able to take day trips to explore the ancient wonders of Granada, Cordoba, Seville, and even—by ferry across the Straits of Gilbraltar—to Tangiers. And they both had a great time.

Without realizing it, Susan and Lois accomplished a classic negotiated settlement of conflict. The key elements in it were:

1). Both parties had a keen interest in reaching agreement, in this case the incentive of reduced travel expenses and companionship rather than "winning" per se.

2). Both parties were willing and able to identify the real goals that lay behind their opening positions, and thus to discover that their highest priority interests were compatible.

3). Both parties were willing to work on a list of alternative settlements that represented in varying proportions their combined real interests.

Once the options list was created, their chance of ultimately reaching agreement was excellent.

HELP!

Needless to say, negotiating the settlement of international disputes is a great deal more difficult than planning a mutually satisfactory vacation.

Where the parties involved are ancient and bitter rivals, the emotional drive for victory or vengeance may make both sides resistant to rational consideration of what their real interests—including the avoidance of bloodbaths—are.

In some cases, it may turn out that the real interests of the disputing parties are genuinely incompatible. If, for instance, the Israelis and the Palestinians both seek not just autonomous, exclusive, and secure homelands, but are actually determined to establish their respective states on the single bit of land to which both peoples are emotionally attached, negotiated settlement is clearly impossible.

Other problems accrue when the need to save face is of genuine interest to both parties—most of the time—and when differences in the cultures of the parties negotiating lead to misunderstandings about the goals or purposes of tactics.

Moreover, many international disputes affect more than just the nations directly involved; other members of alliances or the superpower supporters of the nations negotiating may actively assert their interest in the nature of the settlement.

There is a clear need for skilled "facilitators" who can evenhandedly help the parties in the negotiations work through the conflict-resolution process that Susan and Lois, in their less emotionally charged discussions, were able to come up with by themselves.

There are no formal international mechanisms for providing this kind of aid at present. Although the secretary-general of the United Nations, the pope, and the heads of state or foreign ministers of major powers have often served voluntarily as facilitators of the peaceful resolution of international conflicts, they have done so on an ad hoc basis . . . and only rarely with success.

Superpower intervention is another possibility. As long as direct Soviet involvement is not a factor, the United States has shown a willingness to intervene as a mediator and to work for peaceful resolution of conflict. The Camp David Accord which brought stability and peace to the relationship between Israel and Egypt is a major success story. President Carter was willing to put U.S. prestige on the line and to "sweeten the deal" in order to bring the Sadat and Begin governments to agreement.

In other situations, our mediation efforts have been less successful. Secretary of State Haig's unceasing shuttle diplomacy during the three weeks it took British warships to steam to the South Atlantic was not enough to prevent the war over the Falkland Islands. And the complexities of the Lebanese situation, which involves warring internal factions as well as the Israelis, the Syrians, the Palestine Liberation Organization, *and* the Soviets, have thus far eluded our would-be peacemakers.

COME TOGETHER

CLARITY: I wonder if the situation in the Middle East could be settled once and for all if it were mediated by a team of U.S. and Soviet diplomats, with each superpower exercising its influence to bring the factions with which it is friendly to the negotiating table.

RUPERT: Well, I suppose it could be done if you got the U.S.–Soviet team together, but there's no reason to think that could ever happen.

CLARITY: It may not look too feasible right now, but there are examples of the United States and the Soviet Union working in *tacit* cooperation toward ending a regional conflict.

During the June 1967 Arab-Israeli war, Moscow and Washington communicated repeatedly. While the substance of the dialogue was in part hostile—Kosygin threatened Soviet intervention if the Israelis did not halt military operations and Johnson made it clear that the United States was "prepared to resist

Soviet intrusion"—both of the superpowers pressured their respective allies for an early halt to hostilities.

I'd like to think that with both of the superpowers becoming increasingly aware of the dangers of regional conflicts escalating into nuclear war, we could see this kind of cooperation repeated and expanded to include overtly collaborative peacemaking efforts. Visible cooperation would warn belligerent nations that support from their most powerful allies in warlike behavior could not be counted on, and the spectacle of the United States and the Soviet Union working together for peace could inspire a global recommitment to settlement of disputes through negotiation.

Listen to What the Man Says. The candidates may not want to answer these questions—they're bound to make *somebody* mad whatever they say—but they should be strongly encouraged to do so.

- If you are elected, can you foresee circumstances under which it would be advisable to solicit formal superpower cooperation and consultation in trying to mediate international disputes—especially those that involve nations that are aligned with the superpowers?

- What potential benefits could such cooperation have for the overall U.S.–Soviet relationship?

- Do you think that such a partnership commitment, with each superpower using what influence it has, could help resolve the situation in the Middle East? In Central America?

- What unilateral steps might the United States take to strengthen our ability to resolve international disputes before they escalate to war?

THE IMPOSSIBLE DREAM

The ruinous wars of the twentieth century have attracted greater numbers of the human race to the dream of securing world peace through the collective actions of nations.

In 1914, British Foreign Secretary Sir Edward Grey, frustrated in his attempts to convene an international conference that might keep a series of blunders and misunderstandings from triggering World War I, introduced the concept of an orderly and cooperative global system to prevent such crises in the future. With the active support of President Woodrow Wilson, his concept resulted in the formation of the League of Nations in 1918. But the League, weakened by flaws in its operational design and the isolationist refusal of the United States to join, was unable to halt Japanese, German, and Italian aggression in the 1930s and was dissolved at the outbreak of World War II.

But the dream didn't die. In August of 1941, Roosevelt and Churchill drew up the Atlantic Charter, which both defined their aims in the war and called for the abandonment of war as an instrument of international relations. The following January, twenty-six nations endorsed that principle by signing the Declaration of the United Nations, and in the midst of war the plans for long-term peace moved along quickly.

The United Nations was formally established on October 24, 1945, with a charter that begins, "We, the peoples of the United Nations, determined to save succeeding generations from the scourge of war, which twice in our lifetime has brought untold sorrow to mankind. . . ."

WHO'LL STOP THE RAIN?

Unlike national governments, the United Nations has no strong mechanisms for keeping its members' behavior in check. It has neither the equivalent of a criminal court which can indict, try, punish, and thereby deter misbehavior nor the equivalent of a civil court which can hear the facts and render binding judgments in disputes.

The International Court of Justice, which is the judicial arm of the United Nations, is a major cut above any similar institution of the past. It consists of fifteen justices, no two of whom may be from the same country. But the Court has been totally ineffective as a mechanism for resolving serious international disputes: it can only act when requested to by the nations involved in the dispute, and it has no enforcement power of its own, only the capacity to make recommendations to the United Nations Security Council which is supposed to have that power.

A major problem with the Security Council is that the application of enforcement machinery can be vetoed by any one of the five permanent members—the United States, the Soviet Union, Great Britain, France, and China. So you can be pretty sure that sanctions will never be used against any of *those* nations (which all just happen to be members of the Nuclear Club). Moreover, given the tendency of all the small and medium-size nations to be allied or aligned with one or another of these five nations, it is unlikely that the full Security Council will *ever* vote for enforcement by international military forces. The one time that enforcement was ever applied—against North Korea in 1950—was a fluke. The Soviet Union, which was backing the North Korean invasion of South Korea, had boycotted Security Council meetings because of the seating of the Republic of China rather than the People's Republic of China. Had the Soviet ambassador been present for the vote, he would certainly have vetoed the enforcement action.

In summary, then, the United Nations envisioned in the halcyon days immediately following the Allied victory in World War II simply does not exist. It is, as an American historian once argued, "a child of the Cold War . . . rent asunder by the conflict between East and West."

Listen to What the Man Says. Pay careful attention to how the candidates answer these questions.

- Is there any possibility of converting the United Nations into a credible mechanism for the peaceful resolution of international disputes?

- Should we abandon the United Nations and start all over on a new institution—like the Founding Fathers did when they tossed out the Articles of Confederation and produced the Constitution?

REACH OUT OF THE DARKNESS

Think for Yourself. The notion of moving toward peaceful resolution of international conflicts by increasing mutual understanding only works when the fundamental interests of the nations involved are compatible. It may be pleasantly surprising to discover that your adversaries do not, in fact, have three heads, but that won't take you very far if you're both intent on sole possession of the same plot of land.

We can assume that virtually every nation on this planet, if asked to rank its interests, would put national survival at the very top of the list, with whatever honorable or less-than-honorable intentions it had toward the rest of the world running a distant second.

What approach would you take to get all the nations of the world—the superpowers, other developed nations, and Third World states—to recognize that the global threat of nuclear war constitutes the greatest single threat to their individual survival?

Assuming that you could get all the nations to agree that the survival of any one of them is compatible with the survival of all the others, how would you move them from this admission to the resolution of specific international disputes?

11

DANCE THIS MESS AROUND

How You Can Prevent Nuclear War Through the 1984 Election

Guess what? If you've reached this point without skipping any pages, you have about as good a grasp of "the big picture" of the nuclear war issue as most of the candidates for the presidency! Whether or not you've made up your own mind about which policies are most promising for each of the firebreak issues, you understand how the issues work, and that's enough to get you started.

You should also recognize by now that if you sit on your backside waiting for "somebody" to bring the American electorate into productive confrontation with the nuclear war issue, that may not happen at all.

So roll up your sleeves, and let's get going. Here's what you need to know about the American political system and what you can do in 1984—and well beyond.

WILD WORLD

The bad news about American politics is that it's becoming more of a circus than ever. In the same way that the superpower competition in nuclear weapons doesn't make for sound security, political candidates' competition through artful sloganeering and alarmingly nonsubstantive television commercials doesn't make for sound government which requires that "the folks" and their leaders have thought hard about and agreed upon the general thrust of important policies.

This is not to suggest that politicians are any worse than the rest of us. Indeed, given the well-known rigors and headaches of elective politics and of the public service that follows, we've got to assume that there is some component of idealism in the will to power, some vision of a program that could make things better.

But American politics is a Darwinian universe: one must play the game to win, in accordance with the established rules of pragmatism, or rise nobly above the carnival antics and—nine times out of ten—go down in heroic flames. The problem with choosing the latter course is that whoever does so never has an opportunity to enact the vision he or she started out with. (And the problem with the former course is that the vision tends to fade in the face of "political necessity," but by that time the will to power for its own sake has taken over.)

So serious candidates get Madison Avenue to package them as bright, clear-thinking, witty, humble, compassionate, and/or authoritative, and they get speech writers to produce dramatic monologues of ringing phrases that frequently skirt the substance of the issues. This is merely pragmatism: The less concretely they address a controversial issue, the fewer voters they are likely to alienate. Combine this understanding with a disarming smile, a couple of cute kids, and some nifty one-liners and you've got yourself a winning image.

Politicians are running for office this way because that's what's been working of late, and it works because "we the people" make it work—or, more precisely, let it work. Some of us vote a straight party line, others to throw out whichever rascals are now in, and still others for a vague but extravagant promise, for cute kids, or for an eloquent turn of phrase. Some of us do not vote at all. We haven't even demanded a full explanation of how individually proposed policies would work, much less an analysis of their mutual compatibility.

So you might say that we've gotten what we deserve. If the cumulative effect of U.S. national security policies over the past 38 years is suddenly curdling our blood, we've no one but ourselves to blame.

Fortunately, we are discovering what a terrifying dilemma our cumulative apathy has brought us to just when we're facing a terrific opportunity to get ourselves out of it. In the course of 1983, each day's headlines seemed to increase public awareness of the threat of nuclear war, and naturally, the candidates are already preparing to make national security an important campaign issue. Our challenge is to see that the prevention of nuclear war becomes the *most* important campaign issue, that the debate doesn't deteriorate into slogans and simplistic yes or no answers to the same old questions.

BLESSED BE THE TIES THAT BIND

"A political leader must keep looking over his shoulder all the time to make sure the boys are still there. And if the boys aren't still there, he's no longer a political leader." This real-world truth from the statesman Bernard Baruch points to the *good news* about American politics: beneath their glossy packaging, the people who are in it are still politicians. In an era when one televised speech can make or break them, they are more interested than ever in the time-honored activities of testing the water, floating trial balloons, and groping for the pulse of American public opinion.

So even while they are making television commercials to "communicate" with us, they are using private polls to collect constant feedback about whether we like them, how we feel about various issues, and whether we like their stands on the issues.

And if they discover through polls or other means that a lot of us don't like them because we either don't like their stands on various nuclear war-related issues or don't think they're trying hard enough to let us *know* what those stands are, things happen. Emergency campaign staff meetings are called, some advisors are fired, and the candidates' policy positions become "clarified" as if by magic.

You see, sometimes a candidate for president has to reposition himself so that when he looks over his shoulder, the boys—and the girls—are still there.

LET'S PUT IT ALL TOGETHER

So this is what we know so far about the pragmatism of the political arena in 1984:

1). If they had their druthers, it appears that most of the presidential candidates would address the nuclear war issue with elusive comments about specific weapons systems and arms control proposals. They want people to *like* them, and they know full well that if they provide concrete answers to certain questions—"Do you think deterrence by intimidation will work forever?", "Would you take the initiative to improve relations with the Soviet Union, and if so, how, and if not, why not?", and "What would you do to persuade our allies to stop selling weapons willy-nilly to anyone tall enough to put his money on the counter?"—they're bound to make *somebody* mad.

2). Nonetheless, if their constant public opinion measurements reveal a growing demand for full discussion of all the issues that contribute to the prevention of nuclear war, they will feel compelled to respond accordingly, for fear that *everybody* will be mad if they don't.

It follows that a reasonable first-stage goal for the 1984 presidential election campaign is to create a public demand for the candidates to describe, thoroughly and comprehensively, what they would do to prevent nuclear war if elected our "king" of national security.

This approach has a number of critical assets.

First of all, a full discussion of their respective strategies for preventing nuclear war is sure to generate substantive debate among the candidates. By the time they finish attacking each other's position, we will end up with a detailed list of the benefits, risks, and trade-offs entailed in each policy option for each firebreak issue.

Second, because the mass media cover presidential campaigns so closely, this understanding of the relative merits of the policies proposed by various candidates will reach every American who doesn't literally have his or her head stuck in the ground.

And this process of public education through mass exposure of substantive campaign debate contributes vitally to the resurrection of American democracy as it was originally conceived. Thomas Jefferson spelled it out boldly:

> I know of no safe depository of the ultimate powers of the society but the people themselves; and if we think them not enlightened enough to exercise their control with a wholesome discretion, the remedy is not to take it from them, but to inform their discretion by education.

Finally, getting the candidates to submit their preferred policies for consideration by "the folks" is the necessary first step in reaching a thoughtful public consensus on how the United States government should approach the prevention of nuclear war. The past four years have dramatically demonstrated how this issue, shrouded in myth and misinformation, polarizes the American public. Until there is a full and rational public understanding of our options for survival in the Nuclear Age, there is no possibility of defining a farsighted and broadly supported U.S. government strategy for preventing nuclear war.

REACH OUT AND TOUCH (SOMEBODY'S HAND)

For those of us who believe that the American democratic political system is the most effective mechanism through which to seek a comprehensive long-term strategy for preventing nuclear war, even the task of stimulating public demand for thorough discussion of the issue by the candidates is pretty formidable.

This is what we're up against: In a 1981 public opinion poll conducted by *Newsweek* magazine, nearly *half* of the Americans surveyed checked a box that read "I am concerned about the chances of nuclear war, but I try not to think about it."

Shades of Rupert Vanderkopf (before he encountered Clarity Higgs): How can we reach people who have withdrawn into such a self-delusive cocoon?

Once you examine the three attitudes that underlie this psychological retreat from the reality of the nuclear threat, you'll have a fairly good idea of how to proceed with each.

GOOD VIBRATIONS

A great many Americans shrink from the nuclear war problem because they don't feel they are "qualified" to actively seek new solutions. They see the issue as so complex that only those with expertise in weapons technology or national security theory can deal with it productively.

As you now know and can demonstrate, this is hogwash. Whoever got us into this mess is showing no signs of common-sense ideas for getting us out.

In one-on-one discussions, you can show people how far their common sense will take them on this issue. You can explain where deterrence by intimidation came from and how inadequate it has become, and you can point to the easily comprehensible "fuses and firebreaks" concepts as a promising structure upon which to build a more realistic strategy.

DON'T YA WANNA PLAY THIS GAME NO MORE?

Another large group of Americans are absolutely positive that they can come up with some better ideas than anyone who thinks 50,000 nuclear weapons on this planet somehow constitute security, but they don't think that the political establishment can be made responsive to the concerns and ideas of the American electorate. They have completely lost confidence in the democratic process.

There is, of course, ample reason for disillusionment, but there are also striking examples of grass-roots movements precipitating major changes in U.S. government policy in the past two decades. The most notable of these are the withdrawal of U.S. military forces from Vietnam and the enactment of legislation to protect the quality of our air and water from pollution.

Think of yourself as the initiator of a ripple effect, and explain that effect to the people who need their faith in democracy renewed in the terms of commercial television's pop culture: "I told two friends, and they told two friends, and they told two friends. . . ."

THE WHITE KNIGHT

Perhaps the largest category of Americans who "try not to think about" nuclear war are those who don't quite believe in it at a gut level. These people are the toughest ones to get through to, in part because the reality of nuclear war doesn't quite fit in any of our heads.

The notion of nuclear war is sort of like the notion of spatial infinity: we "believe" in it abstractly, but our very concept of space includes boundaries and we can't quite muster a sense of what infinite space is really *like*. Similarly, we can look at photographs of Hiroshima and Nagasaki in the aftermath of the bombing, but the actual events seem remote in time and space. And the prospect of *full-scale* nuclear war is even less real: However often we quote the numbers, one hundred fifty million American dead is literally inconceivable.

How can you get people to act on an idea that remains largely an abstraction to them? If we reexamine the success of the grass-roots movements mentioned above, we can see that they didn't really take off until the problems they addressed became tangible to the great mass of Americans. It wasn't until virtually every American knew someone whose brother, son, or husband had been in Vietnam that the movement seeking to stop the war became broad-based. And environmentalism was widely viewed as baseless hysteria until the Cuyahoga River caught fire in Cleveland and women in the industrial suburbs of St. Louis found their stockings dissolving on their legs from acids in the air.

But we can't wait for a "tangible demonstration" that nuclear war is a *real* problem. We must bring the great mass of Americans into constructive psychological confrontation with the facts of the issue before it is too late.

And, as we've repeatedly pointed out, "we" is you. To people who shrink from the idea of nuclear war, even the most straightforward organized efforts at public education on the issue may seem suspicious. But within your personal "sphere of influence"—the circle of your family, friends, colleagues, neighbors, and the people in your school or congregation—you have an established standing. These people have come to trust your motives and your judgment, and however reluctant they may otherwise be to learn about nuclear war, they will give you a hearing.

GO TELL IT ON THE MOUNTAIN

Before you start spreading the word and the hope about nuclear war, you should understand its potential liabilities and assets as an issue.

You already know the bad news: A great many Americans would prefer to think that ignoring nuclear war might make it go away. It is simply too frightening, too complicated, too seemingly intractable for them to deal with.

The good news is that once people understand the reality of the threat and the effect a full-scale nuclear war would have on this country, it is fairly easy to persuade them that the search for attaining a workable remedy is very much their candidates' business.

People with safe jobs can be unconcerned about unemployment; people with no children can be unconcerned about the deterioration of public education; but no one who has recognized the growing threat of nuclear war can long maintain that "it's got nothing to do with me."

Still, getting people to confront this issue is tricky, and best undertaken with some guidelines in mind. For starters, don't focus exclusively on the physical effects of nuclear explosions and the imminence of the threat. Instead, introduce the subject of nuclear war as a real threat but one that is preventable by means we can all understand and employ. This isn't just a good tactic; it has the additional advantage of being true.

It's also important to stress that until such time as technological advances allow nuclear weapons to discriminate between Republicans and Democrats, liberals and conservatives, the problem of nuclear war properly transcends partisan and ideological categories. This is not to say that the issue is not sometimes manipulated by politicians from across the political spectrum. Indeed, part of our job is to build a broad-based and unwavering public demand for substantive treatment of the issue; any candidate who refuses to give serious and thoughtful attention to the problem of nuclear war—the most urgent problem of our era—should discover his or her error on election day.

DOES ANYBODY REALLY KNOW WHAT TIME IT IS?

We will repeat here what we've already said and what should be obvious in any case: to work productively toward the goal of creating a public demand for comprehensive and thorough discussion of all of the firebreak issues by the candidates, you do not need to have made up your own mind about which policies are the most promising.

In fact, as you start talking about nuclear war and the firebreaks that can prevent it, you might get a better reception if you *don't* supply your answers to the relevant questions. One of the problems in getting people involved in this issue is that they have been turned off by those who claim to have a single, simple solution to the problem of nuclear war. However, "if we just institute a freeze," "if we just tough it out with the Russians," "if we just deploy MX," are all too pat to be true.

Moreover, once you get your friends talking with you about the various firebreak issues, the resulting exchange of ideas, insights, and information will help you clarify your own views.

BALLROOM BLITZ

Reaching out and talking to people about nuclear war and how it can be prevented is probably as important as anything else you can do to constructively raise the issue in the course of the 1984 campaign, but you may want to do some of the following as well:

• Write letters to the editor of your local paper or a newsmagazine for publication: "Although your coverage of X and Y's recent debate was generally excellent, your analysis failed to note that both candidates side-stepped the issue of how we can engage the Russians in cooperative efforts to stop the flow of arms to the Middle East. . . ."
• Try to interest your local media—especially newspapers—in using the "fuses and firebreaks" concept as a means of thoroughly debriefing the candidates on their strategies for the pre-

vention of nuclear war. You might send a copy of this book to the managing or editorial page editor of your local paper, along with a letter suggesting that the candidates be invited to submit written explanations of their proposed policies on various issues. Candidates who try to gloss over tough questions posed by individuals cannot afford to do so with the media, and your local media might be especially receptive to such a suggestion as your state primaries or caucuses approach.

• You can also trigger some changes by writing to individual candidates: "Dear Senator Slick: As one of your long-time supporters, I am dismayed to see how consistently you have avoided answering questions about how you will seek to involve our allies in strengthening nuclear nonproliferation mechanisms if you are elected president. The threat of nuclear war is clearly the greatest problem of our era, and your refusal to state what you would do to make sure that nuclear weapons stay out of the hands of leaders like Colonel Qaddafi makes me wonder whether you are serious about your candidacy." The candidates' campaign staffs will respond to such initiatives with position papers or letters; more important, they will take note of both the public's interest in a specific issue and of the decreasing likelihood that their candidates will be able to get away with evasions.

DID YOU EVER HAVE TO MAKE UP YOUR MIND?

How can you personally move from an understanding of the individual firebreaks and their respective roles in an overall strategy for preventing nuclear war to deciding for yourself which policy options are the best—something that you'll want to do before you vote?

• As mentioned earlier, the conversations that you have with your friends and colleagues as part of your outreach efforts can be very productive. Comparing notes and concepts will strengthen your understanding of the issues and increase your store of relevant facts.

• The statements of individual candidates on individual issues and what they have to say about each other's positions will be covered in the evening news on an ongoing basis but not very substantively. You'll probably learn more by watching the television programs that offer more intensive coverage and analysis:

the "McNeil-Lehrer Newshour" and "Washington Week in Review" are carried by most PBS stations; CBS has "Face the Nation"; NBC has "Meet the Press"; and ABC has "This Week with David Brinkley."

• You should also make a point of reading weekly newsmagazines. *People* is unlikely to be very helpful, but *Time, Newsweek,* and *U.S. News and World Report* all carry excellent reporting, commentary, and analysis. Similarly, newspapers that focus heavily on national and international news—the *New York Times,* the *Washington Post,* the *Los Angeles Times,* and the *Boston Globe,* for instance—are available by subscription or at newsstands in many cities and in most public libraries.

• In the section called "When You're Hot, You're Hot," we've provided a list of books written specifically for nonexperts. Most of them cover two or more of the most important firebreaks issues with basic facts and clear explanations of concepts. All but one of them are paperbacks or pamphlets that are readily available from bookstores or through the mail.

• In the past several years, lectures, panel discussions, and other opportunities for the public to learn about issues related to nuclear war have increased dramatically in communities across the country. Many of these are sponsored by local colleges, churches, and civic groups and are publicized in local papers or on the radio. Check some of them out, and take a friend or two along with you. You can usually predict whether the presentation will be biased from its title, participants, and sponsoring organizations. If it is you will be prepared to take the proceedings with an appropriate grain of salt. Anything entitled "Our Friend Yuri" or "What the Godless Commies Have in Mind for America" is clearly suspect, but you can always attend to ask questions.

CHANGES IN LATITUDES, CHANGES IN ATTITUDES

When you've satisfied yourself that certain policy positions are clearly more promising than others, you are ready to begin comparing the various candidates' endorsed strategy on each firebreak issue with your own.

It may be that a certain candidate is clearly more in your space than any of the others but not completely. Let him know about it through the mail: "Dear Candidate: I think that you are right on the mark on virtually all of the issues relating to the prevention of nuclear war, but I wish you would show more willingness to lean on our allies to sign the Nuclear Nonproliferation Treaty. I fully understand the reasons that France and Israel give for not doing so, but I am convinced that the French willingness to sell their advanced reactors to some of the most combative governments in the world and the rumored Israeli cooperation with Taiwan are contributing materially to the global danger of nuclear war. Surely France can generate foreign revenue in other ways. And if Israel is being slandered by the rumors, the Israeli government can best prove that by signing the treaty."

Writing such letters is far from futile. Just keep in mind that even the best candidates must remain balloon floaters and pulse takers in order to land the job they're working so hard for. The more we can do to convince *all* the candidates that the new political pragmatism of 1984 lies in thoughtful and coherent policies, rather than in slick commercials, the better our chance of ending up with a national strategy for preventing nuclear war— a strategy that the majority of Americans can support and stick with in the face of progress and setbacks.

TAKIN' IT TO THE STREETS

Once you have decided for yourself that a specific candidate is committed to the most promising overall strategy and to specific policies for preventing nuclear war, go for it.

Talk up your candidate among your friends, pointing to the policies you endorse and mentioning the flaws in the other candidates' programs. Contribute money. Volunteer your time to stuff envelopes or distribute literature door to door. Do whatever else needs to be done. Make sure all your friends are registered to vote.

And vote as if your life depended on it.

12

A TIME-SPACE PERSPECTIVE

Okay, so the prose wasn't always Hemingway and the humor wasn't always Mencken. But did the message get through? Did you get it, or do you still think, as we say at Ground Zero, "It's only nuclear war, right?"

This issue is *so* serious that we've got to work it *real* hard. There is a lot at stake.

What if Carl Sagan and those scientists are right and a nuclear war with as few as 5,000-odd nuclear bombs going off—one-tenth of the planet's current arsenal—could lead to so much dust (as in ashes to ashes . . .) in the atmosphere that we'd have another ice age . . . and find out if our species with all its technology will be any hardier than the dinosaurs. Sure, maybe they're wrong, maybe they're off by a factor of two—or ten? But who wants to run the experiment?

And in the face of this we now "know," with almost absolute certainty, that *we are not alone.*

Yep. E.T. almost certainly exists. The U.S.-British-Dutch infrared Astronomical Satellite has found fifty stars with large amounts of mass; undoubtedly there are planets in orbit around them. And the satellite just got up there three months ago and has just begun to search the sky. That means that if each of the estimated one hundred billion (give or take a few) galaxies in the known universe contains the ball-park figure of one hundred billion stars that are in our Milky Way galaxy, then there are probably googleplexes (one googleplex $= 10^{10}$) of stars with planets.

Marry that to the ongoing research on how life got started on this planet back there four or so billion years ago. All it takes is a molecule that can reproduce itself in the soup of its chemical building blocks! Add a couple zillion evolutionary steps and you get Elvis Presley and he changed all our lives!

And if all it takes is a planet that boils off hydrogen, oxygen, and CO_2 as ours did when it cooled five or so billion years ago, then not only might E.T. exist, he might play tennis like Billy Jean King. And wouldn't that be some Wimbledon.

Or maybe he will be a mile-wide pink fuzzy blob off a planet one hundred times the size of Jupiter with an atmosphere of methane.

Who knows?

But what if E.T. doesn't exist? What if in all those 10^{22} solar systems there ain't nuthin' but gas and rocks. What if there is something so special about this Big Blue Marble that this is it? Think about it.

And what if we queer the deal? What if we snuff it out . . . and it doesn't happen again? What if time moves? What if "history" shows that some twenty billion years after the Big Bang (that's 20 A.B.B.) the life that emerged on planet Earth in the Milky Way came to an abrupt halt? . . . And it never reappeared.

And that is what we're in. Like it or not. Whether it's next year or next millennium you and I, we—*homo sapiens*—have got to end war as a means of resolving national state disputes or we are going to run Sagan's experiment. Deterrence is not going to work forever. If you take no other fact away from this book it should be that wars must eventually go! They must be thrown on the trash heap of history, along with slavery, human sacrifice, colonialism, right of the lords of the manor, primogeniture and the idea that boys are smarter than girls! (Even our Founding Fathers didn't think "they" were fit to vote . . . and the first woman president of the United States is probably now playing hopscotch, or running a city, or maybe riding on shuttles.)

It is already some trash heap and war is the next addition. We've *got* to do it.

Because we may in fact be alone. And we have *got to get out of this place!* This place is doomed! Earth, that is. The scientists say our beloved sun has about five billion years of gusto left and then it's literally going to run out of gas and die.

Oh, it will be some sunset. But where will we be? Will we die with our planet?

Or will we make it? Will we conquer war and watch the death of Earth from some place in the Constellation Andromeda, somewhere in the Crab Nebulae?

That is what is at stake when we talk about preventing nuclear war. We have got to get on with *insuring* that this wonderful miracle we call life goes on—whether it's to be continued here until E.T. arrives or to be carried on by skipping from planet to planet as stars and galaxies come and go.

So let's win the war, eh? You and me. Let's choose life, no matter where it came from or where it's going. Who cares what's on the other side of the Big Bang anyway? We owe it to the moms and dads who got us this far and to the kids who deserve *their* chance to take the ride. And some ride it is.

Appendix

WHEN YOU'RE HOT, YOU'RE HOT
Where to Get More Information
on the Nuclear War Issue

The following books and pamphlets provide hard information on one or more of the firebreak issues in a manner that is unbiased and specifically geared to nonexperts.

Ground Zero. *Nuclear War: What's in It for You?* New York: Pocket Books, 1982. A "primer" providing information on the history of nuclear weapons and the arms race, national security and arms control strategies, the likely effects of nuclear war, and how—if you're so inclined—to make a bomb.

Ground Zero. *What About the Russians—and Nuclear War?* New York: Pocket Books, 1983. Who are the Russians, why are they mad at us, and what is their role in the threat and prevention of nuclear war?

The Harvard Nuclear Study Group. *Living With Nuclear Weapons.* New York: Bantam Books, 1983. Covers our current predicament and what can be done with arms control and nonproliferation efforts.

Jacobsen, Carl G. *The Nuclear Era: Its History, Its Implications.* Cambridge, MA: Oelgeschlager, Gunn & Hain, 1982. A well-researched and interestingly written presentation of the dynamics of the U.S.–Soviet competition, strategies, nonproliferation, and arms control.

League of Women Voters Education Fund. *The Quest for Arms Control: Why and How.* Washington: League of Women Voters of the United States, 1983. Covers objectives, history, and criteria of nuclear arms control agreements.

Meyer, Tina. *Understanding Nuclear Weapons and Arms Control.* Arlington, VA: Arms Control Research, 1983. Well-defined terms and basic numbers on U.S. nuclear strategy, the current U.S. and Soviet nuclear arsenals, and arms control agreements.

The following book is one you should keep around to remind you of what is at stake when you feel your energy faltering and your concentration slipping.

Schell, Jonathan. *The Fate of the Earth.* New York: Knopf, 1982. (Also available in Avon paperback.) An eloquent and compelling exploration of the problem of nuclear war and the possibility of extinction.

NOTES

NOTES